AN ANARCHIST'S MANIFESTO

Warbler Press

ISBN 978-1-7360628-2-1 (paperback)
ISBN 978-1-7360628-3-8 (e-book)

warblerpress.com

Acclaim for *An Anarchist's Manifesto*

"Anarchy—free cooperation among equals—is a principle of everyday life. It also shapes disobedient communities' struggles against oppression, looking forward to a social order without rulers or classes. Glenn Wallis writes down to earth and up to the minute, a manifesto in the best tradition of Emma Goldman and Colin Ward. If you are not an anarchist (yet?)—this book is for you."

—Uri Gordon, author of *Anarchy, State and Revolution* and *Anarchy Alive!*

"In this seductive stroll through the realms of philosophy, history, and everyday life, Wallis guides the curious toward a meeting with anarchy—one of today's most powerful but maligned political convictions. Whether it leads you to raise a black flag or merely to raise an eyebrow, *An Anarchist's Manifesto* will leave you with little doubt about which side you're on."

—ak thompson, author of *Premonitions: Selected Essays on the Culture of Revolt*

"Glenn Wallis's anarchist manifesto is a gentle, undogmatic exploration of anarchist practice. It explains how an anarchist articulation of shared values can transform failing democratic institutions and unjust systems of organization. This is not a conventional manifesto: there is no elaborate policy program or list of empty promises. It calls for the recovery of an anarchist sensibility as the bulwark against relentless capitalist exploitation and corrupt, lawless government."

—Ruth Kinna, member of the Anarchism Research Group at Loughborough University UK, former co-convenor of the Anarchist Studies Network and co-editor of the journal *Anarchist Studies*

"Read this manifesto. Wallis convincingly argues that anarchism is an 'ungrand tradition' of ordinary people engaging in concrete communism, practiced in societies against the state and as well as in exilic spaces at the edges of capitalism. These spaces are not 'somewhere else,' they are everywhere around us, in the interstices of the dominant society."

—Andrej Grubačić, Professor of Anarchist Anthropology, CIIS-San Francisco

"This lucid and incisive manifesto—in the full force of the term—provides a clear articulation of anarchism: what it is, what it is not, and why it is our best chance at reclaiming our world from the ravages of capitalism, exploitation, and authoritarianism. Glenn Wallis's *An Anarchist's Manifesto* is unflinchingly committed to an anarchist worldview, a worldview in which anarchism as what Wallis calls a 'certain way of being' engenders mutually aiding relations between people. Refusing hierarchy, oppression, coercion, and exploitation, *An Anarchist's Manifesto* is concerned, first and foremost, with acting on and changing the world. This is not starry-eyed utopianism; this is anarchism, the way to a more just world."

—Marquis Bey, African American Studies and English professor, Northwestern University

"This engaging but scholarly book will appeal to both anarchist activists and readers curious about what anarchism can offer to contemporary political struggles. While not shying away from posing and exploring tough questions, Wallis offers his readers a wealth of intellectual resources and inspiring historical and contemporary examples of anarchist praxis. His impassioned manifesto both argues and demonstrates that anarchism is, above all, 'a way of being in the world.'"

—Judith Suissa, Professor of Philosophy of Education, University College London, Institute of Education

"Glenn Wallis's *Manifesto* presents a powerful, eloquent, and eminently practical case for anarchism. This is a book that one could very usefully pass on to a neighbor, if that neighbor is inspired by values like love, respect, care, mutual aid, sharing, equality, and freedom. The book will win over many through its simple and profound message that 'anarchy' is in no way alien to ordinary people, but is, rather, something that we find in the most admirable ideals and practices all around us. Wallis shows that 'a better world is possible' because it is and has been quite actual—at many points in history, in many places today, and most significantly, in our own lives."

—John Clark, author of *The Impossible Community: Realizing Communitarian Anarchism* and *Between Earth and Empire: From the Necrocene to the Beloved Community*

AN ANARCHIST'S MANIFESTO

GLENN WALLIS

I dedicate this manifesto to the memory of Peter Frank.
The free school that Peter created near Philadelphia in the 1970s was permeated by the values advocated in this work. As his student, I absorbed those values. For that, my gratitude is boundless.

The impossible is the least that one can demand.

—James Baldwin

CONTENTS

1.
Are You Already an Anarchist?

When driving in traffic, do you take care to avoid accidents? What about in a grocery store? Do you navigate your shopping cart cautiously through the crowded aisles, and wait your turn (however impatiently) in the checkout line? Going through the security check at the airport can be very aggravating. Do you nonetheless inch forward with everyone else, place your shoes on the conveyer belt, and walk through the security station? If you do all of this *not* out of a sense of duty and deference or mere respect for the law, but because you desire to contribute to the smooth operation of the shared, collective task at hand, then you already cherish two central values of an anarchist way of life: order and cooperation.

Do you actively strive, wherever possible, to help out family, friends, neighbors, work associates, maybe even strangers? Would you expect the same from them if you were in need? Do you have this attitude *not* out of a sense of obligation, guilt, indebtedness, or *quid pro quo* insurance, but because of a sense of interdependent connection with others? If so, you already cherish the central anarchist value of mutual support.

Imagine that you're in a discussion, say, in a classroom with fellow students, around a dinner table with a group of friends, or at a conference table with colleagues at work. Do you believe that, in such situations, people are more likely to express their views in engaged, creative, and perhaps even bold ways if no overshadowing authority figure is present (for example, the teacher, a mansplaining male, the boss)? If you believe that groups of people are capable of intelligently determining matters on their own, without the need of a coercive figure, then you possess the crucial anarchist dispositions of being anti-authoritarian and anti-hierarchical, or, positively expressed, egalitarian.

Do you believe that all people should be granted every privilege and access afforded the most advantaged members of society? Do you believe that protection and dignity should be extended to animals? Do you believe that we should treat the environment with the utmost care? If so, you share the anarchist conviction that we must strive to eliminate all forms of domination.

On reflection, do you believe that the problems illustrated here are the result *not* merely of individual belief and behavior, but of larger structures, such as families, neighborhoods, schools, workplaces, economic systems, and society as a whole? For example, at the very moment I am beginning this text (summer 2020), more and more people are expressing the view that eliminating racism should no longer be considered a matter of changing people's opinion about black people. Racism in America, this view goes, does not exist in this or that private head. It exists in a vast network of shared imagery—on the internet, on television, in movies, advertising, the nightly news, and literature—often extending back decades and even centuries: the black person as poor, uneducated, angry, violent, or sexually voracious. Racism exists in the damaging metaphors and tropes embedded in our ordinary, everyday, perfectly acceptable language usage: a dark mark on a person's reputation; the black stain of a nation's history; a black soul, dark thoughts, dark humor, a dark future, a dark (metaphorical) cloud, a dark outlook or forecast, dark despair, a literal and figurative dark horse; black knight; blackguard; a dark political speech; the dark web (of illicit activity); the black sites set up as secret illegal interrogation sites for terror suspects; black market, blacklist, black out, black magic, blackball, blackmail, black sheep. While not all of these terms have roots in our racist past in the same way that "darkey" or "black Barbie" do, their invariably negative meanings contribute to racial stereotyping. We could continue in this fashion indefinitely. We could, moreover, perform the same kind of broad social analysis for patriarchy and misogyny, anti-LGBTQ views, and views toward animals and the environment. If you believe that such an analysis, and that *only* such an analysis, is capable of getting to the heart of the matter, than you share two essential, interrelated anarchist views: material structures have formative primacy over an individual's consciousness; and thus, to change the world we must first of all change these structures.

Do you believe that the government is made up, to a consequential extent, of a class of people with vested interests in protecting one another's wealth, advantage, influence, and privilege? Do you believe that this ruling class values profit over people, in particular the profits of corporations over the wellbeing of the very people in whose name they govern? Do you believe that this class of people should be irrevocably removed from power, and that, in principle, "the people" be free to create mechanisms for direct democracy, unencumbered by corporate interests? If so, you embrace the animating spirit of anarchism: the state is a major part of the problem, and its converse, stateless governance is a major part of the solution.

Finally, do you believe that the structures I have mentioned here, including those of the government and corporations, are inextricably bound up in the all-pervasive social, political, economic, even psychological, formation known as "capitalism?" Do you therefore conclude that, at this moment in time, capitalism itself is at the root of our most pressing problems—political divisiveness, corporate plunder of resources, widespread hunger and poverty and deprivation, racism, misogyny, and countless other varieties of oppression, environmental devastation, unspeakable animal cruelty, and perpetual warfare? If so, you stand, with those on the far left of the political spectrum, and possibly with anarchists, who hold the conviction that no less than the complete abolishment of capitalism is required for any change worthy of the name to unfold.

If you are not already a confirmed anarchist, I am hoping to catalyze in you several realizations regarding anarchism. In short, the following principles can be extrapolated. At its core, anarchism is decidedly ungrand. Most essentially, it is an approach to living in community with other people, animals, and the natural world. Asking you to picture anarchism happening in the grocery store or at a traffic light might seem trivial; but the purpose is to suggest an image of anarchists drastically different from the one we commonly see: black-clad hoodlums rampaging through our city streets, smashing windows and setting fire to Starbucks. That image, of course, is not wholly unjustified. Such acts have been carried out in the name of anarchism. But to engage it as the dominant image in your awareness is akin to picturing a camo-clad, M249 automatic weapon-toting member of the United States Marine Corps Ambush Unit as a prototypical advocate of western-style democracy. Both figures operate far removed from the daily unfolding of their respective value systems. (And if you view the former figure as extreme, how do you view the latter?) So, I hope this exercise stimulates in you an image of an anarchist as, principally, a person who holds to, and acts on, certain values. At the same time, I hope to enable you to see that the values and actions of an anarchist, just like those of, say, a liberal democrat or conservative republican, have the potential of extending indefinitely outwards, further and further, ever more deeply into our shared daily interactions, and into the very institutions—family, friendship, neighborhood, school, work, local government, society—that make up our common world.

WHAT IS ANARCHISM?

Why a manifesto[1]? And why anarchist? The desire driving this text is to bring into light a certain *way of being* that history has made opaque. The root meaning of the term *manifesto*, from Latin *manifestum*, is "to

---

1 If you are already a confirmed anarchist, I would recommend a doctrinal-historical overview of anarchism, not a manifesto. For instance, Peter Marshall, *Demanding the Impossible: A History of Anarchism* (Oakland: PM Press, 1991).

make clear or conspicuous"—an apt form for this desire to take. *An Anarchist's Manifesto* is written with a dual purpose in mind. The first purpose is to elucidate the ideas and practices that inform the way of being that goes by this name. I can offer two preliminary definitions to convey a sense of the spirit of this way of life. But before I do, I think it is important to state clearly what anarchism, contrary to popular perception, is *not*. Anarchism is not: (a.) absence of government (although, as we will see, its conception of government is better termed as "self-governance," "free association," or "stateless government"); (b.) a state of lawlessness or political disorder due to the absence of a governing mechanism; (c.) a utopian society of individuals who enjoy complete freedom devoid of governing principles. So, the following will be our working definitions: (i.) *Anarchism: A value system for organizing relations between people. It emphasizes order, cooperation, equality, and mutual support. It rejects authoritarianism, oppression, exploitation, coercion, and hierarchy.* (ii.) *Anarchist: A person who applies and advances the values of anarchism within micro, meso, or macro levels of interaction, that is, from partnerships and small groups to organizations, institutions, and large-scale political formations.* The second, more important purpose, is to convince my readers of the value of anarchism for their own lives. That points to my larger goal, and to the reason that this is written as a manifesto; namely, to bring these anarchist principles into ever-increasing circulation within the personal and institutional relations that create the contours of our shared world.

MY READER

Although I do not always explicitly refer to "you" in the text, I am making assumptions about who you, the reader, are. As the reader of a text titled *An Anarchist's Manifesto*, you are, quite possibly, already fairly left-leaning in your politics and worldview. My hunch is that most of you identify as liberal, but are curious to know what is brewing much farther to your left. (To avoid belaboring the point, let's think of "liberal" in the sense that the term is used colloquially today.[2]) This curiosity is particularly likely given the resurgence of socialism on the American political scene, or at least of what counts as socialism among a conservative electorate. Maybe your curiosity is rooted in dispositions that John Dewey said were common in liberals, namely, "liberality and generosity, especially of mind and character."[3] I would also expect that many of you are deeply concerned with, maybe even actively involved in, issues that are caricatured in certain quarters as being those of the "bleeding-heart liberal" or, more recently, of the "social justice warrior." For these reasons, I think you will find many of the ideas in this manifesto not only attractive, but worthy of application in your own life.

In the laying-bare spirit of a manifesto, I feel compelled to mention another, less generous, assumption that I am making about my reader. Dewey adds to his definition of the term liberal that "It points to an open mind, to emancipation from bigotry and from domination by prejudice." What a wonderful thing that would be! Given what we now know about the phenomenon of implicit bias, however, it is naïve. Dewey admits as much when he adds that his definition applies to "moral attitudes and aspirations."[4] Attitudes are cognitive "as ifs," and aspirations are unrealized ideals. By definition, they have not yet fully materialized as decisive actions in the lived theater of one's life. Rather, their force arguably manifests primarily as factors in the "conflicted soul" of contemporary American liberalism.[5] I will leave it to my readers to reflect on the specific nature of this conflict. I personally suspect that, at heart, is has to do with the fact that "Anarchism is democracy

---

2 See Helena Rosenblatt, *The Lost History of Liberalism: From Ancient Rome to the Twenty-First Century* (Princeton: Princeton University Press, 2018).

3 John Dewey, "The Meaning of the Term: Liberalism," in *The Collected Works of John Dewey: Volume 14, 1939–1941: Essays, Reviews, and Miscellany*, ed. Jo Ann Boydston (Carbondale: Southern Illinois University, 1988), 253.

4 Dewey, "The Meaning," 252.

5 See, Warren Breckman, "The Conflicted Soul of Modern Liberalism," *The New Republic*. Accessed May 1, 2020, https://newrepublic.com/article/152935/conflicted-soul-modern-liberalism.

taken seriously," as Edward Abbey puts it.[6] A liberal is nothing if not a champion of democracy, right? The institutional center of American liberalism is, after all, the Democratic Party. The conflict that I observe in my liberal friends and acquaintances concerns precisely the necessary features of democracy, whether in the micro spheres of our everyday relations or the macro sphere of politics and society. Abbey again gets to the heart of this issue when he writes:

> Anarchism is not a romantic fable, but the hardheaded realization, based on five thousand years of experience, that we cannot entrust the management of our lives to kings, priests, politicians, generals, and county commissioners.

If you believe in the necessity of institutionally-mandated hierarchy and authority for the orderly functioning of our communal lives, then you remain on the side of the political continuum that runs from state communism, through classical liberalism, all the way to totalitarianism and fascism.[7] It will be very, very difficult to convince you that, as anarchists claim, such representative "democracy" invariably leads to *disorder*, and, in its wake, oppression, violence, inequality, and all the rest. The difficulty that I am faced with can be discerned in two communications that I recently received. The first one goes:

> In an email exchange with faculty, I suggested that we should be open to proposals to democratize the university,

---

6 Edward Abbey, *One Life at a Time, Please* (New York: Henry Holt and Company, 1978), 26. Abbey's statement is not as flippant as it may appear. Democracy is formed from Greek *demos*, people, and *kratein*, power, or governing power; so, people power. The various -archy-s—hierarchy, plutarchy, patriarchy, monarchy, etc.—derive from *archia*, which in turn derives from *archon*, top ruler (magistrate).

7 Although it is saturated with acrimony, there actually exists a discussion about liberalism's genealogical relationship to fascist ideology. In a dismissive review of a book she "is not likely to" read (!)—Jonah Goldberg's *Liberal Fascism: The Secret History of the American Left, From Mussolini to the Politics of Meaning*—Megan McArdle can nonetheless write "it seems clear that the intellectual heritage of fascism is at least 50% from the left." See, "Liberal = Fascist?," *The Atlantic*, https://www.theatlantic.com/business/archive/2008/01/liberal-fascist/2598. Accessed June 30, 2020.

> and received the following response from a tenured "radical": "Oh A., please. Don't be so dramatic."

The belief that we must entrust our lives to "county commissioners" to ensure that anything of consequence gets done is not the self-evident fact that the tenured "radical" professor seems to believe it is. It is, in fact, a deeply-rooted prejudice. I will try to disabuse you of it. An even more pernicious prejudice that I cautiously assume for many of my readers can be gleaned from the second communication. It concerns Abbey's rebuttal of the "romantic fable" notion. The message: "Don't worry, your secret is safe with me. I'll keep it on the down-low so as not to damage your street cred with the anarchists." The "secret" is that my wife is an executive administrator in higher education. Numerous deep-seated prejudices are embedded in this communication. For example, apparently lingering in the imagination of the message writer is the late-nineteenth-century caricature of anarchists as poor, uneducated rabble-rousers driven to the anarchist extreme through utter deprivation. Like all caricatures, there is a slither of truth in that image. But the generalizing nature of it is like insisting you have no claim to the values of American democracy or republicanism unless you are indistinguishable from the grimy yeomen and humble craftsmen who made up the "rabble" of George Washington's Continental Army. The notion belies a certain reverse classism: only the disenfranchised have a legitimate claim to radical politics. The fact is, from its inception in 1840 to the present day, anarchism has included in its ranks not only struggling laborers, but every station of life from plumber to professor to prince. What is it about a worldview espousing universal equality that has people like our message writer consigning it to "the street," and all the lowliness that that term implies? I mention this communication here because, throughout my life, I have been exposed to much too much evidence that this caricature is the deeply-ingrained norm. I will try to disabuse you of it.

Ultimately, of course, I do not know who "you" are, what your political leanings are, or what your worldview holds. So, I would, finally, like to introduce an important conceit that will allow me to meaningfully retain the implied or explicit familiar second person address: "you" names a model reader. According to literary theorist and novelist Umberto Eco, a model reader is "a sort of ideal type whom the text not only foresees as a collaborator but also tries to create." That is, the ideas presented in this text constitute a kind of prototype of subjectivity, or personhood. This model reader is an *implicit* reader, existing virtually within the linguistic and conceptual signals that constitute the text. This reader is one who is eager to experiment with, to *use*, the ideas in empirical, explicit, life.[8] It is to that dramatic end, after all, that someone like me writes a *manifesto*.

8 Umberto Eco, *Six Walks in the Fictional Woods* (Cambridge, Mass: Harvard University Press,), 9,

2.
A Simple Idea

At the very root of *anarchy* is a simple idea: social organization without (*an*) a dominating figure or controller (*archos*). Though simple, realizing such a form in our daily lives is virtually impossible.[9] Though virtually impossible, this idea, when pursued, is profoundly constructive. The mere removal of authority has real-world consequences that are in equal measure transformative and far-reaching, for both the individuals involved and society as a whole. That removal catalyzes an array of additional values and ways of being. I was exposed to anarchist principles in action when I attended a "free" school as a teenager.[10] Although we did not always explicitly use the parlance of anarchist theory, my mere participation in the school *exposed* me, in the deepest epidemiological sense of that word, to the practices, the ways of being, that we will be exploring in this text. Once I experienced the creativity and intelligence that are unleashed through, say, mutual cooperation, I could never again value or respect top-down authority. Because of my experience, I have been perplexed that anarchism has remained so marginalized for so long. Indeed, as I learned back then, many exceptionally thoughtful and creative people who are not generally known as

---

9 "Impossible," that is, in the sense of what John Clark calls "Possible Impossibilities:" "Possible Impossibilities include things that are possible only in 'another world' beyond the present system of social determination and social domination." See John Clark, *The Impossible Community: Realizing Communitarian Anarchism* (New York: Bloomsbury Academic, 2013), 2.

10 See page 112. *Free Schools.*

anarchists, or indeed who do not even identify as anarchist, have in fact argued that for humanity to have a future, or at least a future worth living, something like anarchism must become the norm.[11] Why would they think so? More importantly, why might you come to think so? In the following sections, I will say what I, the "anarchist" in the title of the text, have come to understand by the this simple idea. To that end, we will further consider our definitions:

> Anarchism: A value system for organizing relations between people. It emphasizes order, cooperation, equality, and mutual support. It rejects authoritarianism, oppression, exploitation, coercion, and hierarchy.
>
> Anarchist: A person who applies and advances the values of anarchism within micro, meso, or macro levels of interaction; that is, from partnerships and small groups to organizations, institutions, and large-scale political formations.

PRACTICE

In the following sections, I will discuss the main terms of the first definition, and give examples to illustrate the second. The reason that I am taking this approach is because anarchism is nothing if not, in the parlance of the left, a praxis. Basically, this is a German word for "practice." However, it is useful for articulating a specific understanding of both the role of, and the relationship between, theory and practice in shaping our world. And it is very important for understanding the nature of anarchism. In its socialist sense, the concept praxis originates in Marx's *Theses on Feuerbach*. These were notes that Marx jotted down as an exile in Brussels in 1845 as he was turning away from abstract

11 For example, Helen Keller, Oscar Wilde, Ursula Le Guin, Noam Chomsky, Charlie Chaplin, Leo Tolstoy, J.R.R. Tolkien, Henry David Thoreau, John Cage, Edward Abbey, Albert Camus, John Lennon, Bertrand Russell, Dorothy Day, Paul Goodman, Björk, just to get the list started.

idealist notions of being in the world, and toward a deeply embodied materialism. What this means exactly should become clear as we proceed. The gist of the idea is discernible from the first *Thesis*: "The chief defect of all hitherto existing materialism...is that the thing, reality, sensuousness, is conceived only in the form of the *object of contemplation*, but not as *sensuous human activity, practice* [German: *Praxis*], not subjectively." Marx is positing that sensuous human activity is *already* present within the very process of "contemplation," or indeed, in the very creation of the object or idea under consideration. The *Theses* want to place the primacy of praxis—our lived engagement with, and influence on, our social world—over abstraction, or mere "scholastic" approaches to the person in the world that circumvent this engagement.

> People must prove the truth—i.e. the reality and power, the this-sidedness of their thinking, in practice. The dispute over the reality or non-reality of thinking that is isolated from practice is a purely *scholastic* question...All social life is essentially practical. All mysteries which lead theory to mysticism find their rational solution in human practice and in the comprehension of this practice...The philosophers have only interpreted the world, in various ways; the point is to change it.[12]

Praxis thus has two facets. The first facet involves committed action in and on our social formations, and does so, moreover, on the premise that those formations *already* and *continuously* bear our shaping influence. Existing social formations are viewed *not* as natural and inevitable outcomes, but rather as the current result of certain complex processes, primarily historical, cultural, political, and economic in nature. The second facet assumes that *theorizing* different social formations is intertwined in the practical facet. Anarchist bestselling author, Ursula Le Guin (1929–2018), brought this facet to life in her

---

12 Karl Marx, *Theses on Feuerbach*, 1, 2, 8, 11. https://www.marxists.org/archive/marx/works/1845/theses/theses.htm. Accessed May 27, 2020.

National Book Award speech, in which she said: "We live in capitalism, its power seems inescapable—but then, so did the divine right of kings. Any human power can be resisted and changed by human beings. Resistance and change often begin in art."[13] When Marx made his famous proclamation about the philosophers in the last of the *Theses*, he was not asking us to forego theoretical speculation, or, indeed, art. Rather, he assumed the value and promise held out by such work. It is, however, never enough. Praxis is a useful term because it combines two interpenetrated modes of practical action that we typically hold apart: theory and practice. In short, then, praxis names the simultaneous and symbiotic relationship between theoretically-informed practical action and practice-informed theorization. It means: theory in action; action in theorizing. As Marquis Bey puts it, since:

> praxis is a doing, an agential enactment that bears on sociality, then a critical praxis marks an interrogative social enactment. What kind of politics might this lead to? What kind of world might this engender, and who might show up to this promiscuous gathering?[14]

So, again, anarchism is based on a simple proposition. Its ideal is virtually impossible to realize because of the many powerful forces that lead to and perpetuate the status quo, the current state of affairs (indistinguishable from the affairs of the state). Anarchist praxis is nonetheless profoundly constructive because in acting on the world with its values, we give shape, to whatever extent, to a new world. It is important to keep this point in mind as we proceed. For one thing, it puts the lie to the common reputation of anarchism as a starry-eyed utopianism. As a praxis, anarchism is nothing if not a committed and often impassioned experimentation, in thought and action, concerning

---

13 *The Guardian*, "Ursula Le Guin's speech at the National Book Awards: 'Books aren't just commodities.'" https://www.theguardian.com/books/2014/nov/20/ursula-k-le-guin-national-book-awards-speech. Accessed May 27, 2020.

14 Marquis Bey, *Anarcho-Blackness: Notes Toward a Black Anarchism* (Chico: AK Press, 2020), 38-39.

better ways of living together. More importantly, this point puts the onus on everyone who sees the value here to actualize, to whatever extent they are able, the forms of organization they want to see manifest in the world. Anarchism, that is to say, is a set of ideas with which *to do something*. Even more to the point, anarchism is something that is *done*. As Albert Meltzer (1920–1996) insists, anarchism is "a creed that has been worked out in practice rather than from a philosophy."[15]

Before we move on, we should further consider this notion of *extent*. This is actually a somewhat vexed issue in anarchist discourse. A discussion at the outset should help you in imagining how you might employ the ideas in this text.

For anarchism to be realized, must it occur at the *macro* level of what we call nations and states? Much anarchist thought seems to assume so. This strand of thought often reads like political science, offering a theory of the (stateless) state on a grand scale. It concerns itself with uppercase Society. Errico Malatesta's (1853–1932) "The Anarchist Revolution" is pervaded by this spirit of total revolution.

> The revolution is the creation of new living institutions, new groupings, new social relationships; it is the destruction of privileges and monopolies. Revolution is the organization of all public services by those who work in them in their own interest as well as the public's. Revolution is the forming and disbanding of thousands of representative, district, communal, regional, national bodies…Anarchy cannot be achieved until after the revolution, which will sweep away the first material obstacles.[16]

Macro-scale anarchism often includes detailed descriptions of

15 Albert Meltzer, "Anarchism: Arguments for and Against," Introduction, http://www.spunk.org/texts/writers/meltzer/sp001500.html. Accessed May 27, 2020.

16 Errico Malatesta, "The Anarchist Revolution," *The Anarchist Library*, https://theanarchistlibrary.org/library/errico-malatesta-the-anarchist-revolution. Accessed May 28, 2020.

how things will look "under anarchism."[17] It is this proclivity to think through eminently practical matters like money, organization and governance, work and industry, transportation, technology, and so on *ad infinitum*, that contributes to anarchism's reputation as a dreamy utopianism. And yet, is it not reasonable to conclude that until we replace the demonstrably unjust systems of organization that make up our world nothing of consequence will ever change? Some anarchists see that as an unreasonable assertion. Even the fiery Malatesta ends his call to total revolution with these words: "If we are unable to overthrow capitalism, we shall have to demand for ourselves and for all who want it, the right of free access to the necessary means of production to maintain an independent existence." Does "The Anarchist Revolution" end with a submissive flinch?

So, maybe it is enough to realize anarchist ideals at the *micro* level of personal relations and lowercase society. Socialist historian Howard Zinn cautioned against the "grand, heroic actions" that many anarchists associate with macro revolutionary social praxis.

> Revolutionary change does not come as one cataclysmic moment...but as an endless succession of surprises, moving zigzag toward a more perfect society. We don't have to engage in grand, heroic actions to participate in the process of change. Small acts, when multiplied by millions of people, can transform the world.[18]

If we take a sober assessment of the inconceivably gargantuan mobilization of people, power, and material resources required to achieve anything resembling a "revolution," do we not arrive at a similar conclusion? Even a dyed-in-the-wool communist like Slavoj Žižek (or was it Marxist theorist Fredric Jameson?) can proclaim, "it is easier

---

17 Peter Kropotkin's (1842-1921) *The Conquest of Bread* is a good example of this genre. *The Anarchist Library*, https://theanarchistlibrary.org/library/petr-kropotkin-the-conquest-of-bread. Accessed May 28, 2020.

18 Quoted in Cindy Milstein, *Anarchism and its Aspirations* (Chico: AK Press, 2010), 65.

to imagine an end to the world than an end to capitalism."[19] Many leftist thinkers today, in fact, express a similar resignation toward what they view as the vampiric, zombie-like capacities of capitalism, and all of the accompanying political, cultural, and economic modes of life encapsulated in that term. Adapting a term used by German pop artists in the 1960s to parody socialist realism, Mark Fisher names this phenomenon "capitalist realism." This is "the widespread sense that not only is capitalism the only viable political and economic system, but also that it is now impossible even to imagine a coherent alternative to it."[20] The reason for our failure of imagination is that capitalism appears so fundamentally necessary, natural, and inevitable that we lose sight of the fact that it is, like Ursula Le Guin's divine right of kings, a wholly contingent affair. It is, says Fisher,

> more like a pervasive atmosphere, conditioning not only the production of culture but also the regulation of work and education, and acting as a kind of invisible barrier constraining thought and action.

Like the Golem of medieval Jewish lore, capitalism is a deaf and dumb beast fashioned from the dust—created *by humans*—that eventually comes to terrorize its mesmerized makers. Rabbi Zeira was acting as an insurgent anarchist when he confronted the Golem, bellowing, "You were created by the sages; return to your dust!"[21]

But, of course, in real life, the Golem does not return to its dust at our command. If anything, the massive structures of oppression that macro-oriented anarchists intend to destroy only harden over time. In fact, as a recent Monmouth University poll on Americans' views on socialism vs. capitalism indicate, those ostensibly oppressive structures

19 Quoted in Mark Fisher, *Capitalist Realism: Is There No Alternative?* (Winchester: Zero Books, 2009), 2.

20 Fisher, *Capitalist Realism*, 2.

21 *Sefaria*, "Sources in Judaism: Demons, Golems, and Evil Spirits," ¶ 23, https://www.sefaria.org/sheets/84998?lang=en. Accessed May 28, 2020.

resolutely retain their popularity over time.[22] So, to some anarchists, Zinn's "small acts" strategy amounts to a resignation or surrender. Some have rendered even harsher judgements. Murray Bookchin (1921–2006) derisively called this phenomenon "lifestyle anarchism."[23] He contends that anarchists have failed in their efforts at macro change largely because "thousands of self-styled anarchists have slowly surrendered the social core of anarchist ideas to the all-pervasive Yuppie and New Age personalism that marks this decadent, bourgeoisified era." And by "personalism," Bookchin means the individual-preference motivated "small acts" of Zinn's statement. To other anarchists, the "small acts" argument amounts to magical thinking. What guarantee is there that anyone, much less "millions of people," will join my efforts? And even if they do, history predicts that the state would eventually intervene to quash it, and capitalism would find a way to co-opt, commodify, and depotentialize it. Hence, argue the macroists, the necessity for total revolution, which, by definition, dismantles the overarching oppressive infrastructure—the state and capitalism—itself. To which the chorus solemnly intones: That is just not possible. And around and around we go.

Finally, the "extent" of application for anarchist principles might occur at the *meso* level of social organization. I understand the two complementary principles of prefiguration and concrete utopia to be models for this *meso* level anarchism. These ideas are encapsulated in the motto of the Industrial Workers of the World (IWW), the revolutionary international labor union known as the Wobblies: "building the new society in the shell of the old." Urban planner, architect,

22 Monmouth University, "Socialism vs. Capitalism," with the telling subheading: "Socialism not seen as compatible with American values, but opinion is not overwhelmingly negative." https://www.monmouth.edu/polling-institute/reports/monmouthpoll_us_050619. Accessed May 28, 2020.

23 Murray Bookchin, "Social Anarchism or Lifestyle Anarchism: An Unbridgeable Chasm," https://libcom.org/library/social-anarchism--lifestyle-anarchism-murray-bookchin. Accessed May 28, 2020. Bob Black wrote a scathing response to Bookchim in "Anarchy after Leftism," https://theanarchistlibrary.org/library/bob-black-anarchy-after-leftism. Accessed May 28, 2020.

and eminently practical anarchist theorist, Colin Ward (1924–2010), echoes this contention in his often-cited insistence that "If you want to build a free society, the parts are all at hand."[24] Traditionally, this approach calls for praxis within the existing institutions of our social life, such as schools, neighborhood assemblies, businesses, universities, and so on. More recently it has also come to mean the creation of *new* formations of the same, often called "counter-institutions." The assumption is that prefiguration entails the very "embodiment, within the ongoing political practice of a movement, of those forms of social relations, decision-making, culture, and human experience that are the ultimate goal."[25] If the "small acts" approach is, as a popular meme puts it, "being the change you wish to see," prefiguration is "building the models you wish to see," creating the school, business, organization that you wish to see emulated and proliferated in the world. As political scientist Carl Boggs, who popularized this usage of the term in 1977, says of prefiguration:

> Only popular institutions in every sphere of daily existence, where democratic impulses can be most completely realized, can fight off the repressive incursions of bureaucratic centralism and activate collective involvement that is the life-force of revolutionary practice.

At this meso-level, anarchist society originates in the very *doing* of anarchism in, moreover, the very places where individuals form into community. Macro-level anarchists, with a vigilant eye on class struggle and total revolution, might accuse this approach of being a "nonviolent, bourgeois, sanitized anarchism,"[26] but if I want to get anywhere with my readers I will have to take that risk. I believe that the "life-force" of anarchism may manifest either in micro-level

24 Colin Ward, *Anarchy in Action* (London: George Allen & Unwin, Ltd., 1973), 13.
25 Carl Boggs, "Marxism, Prefigurative Communism, and the Problem of Workers' Control," https://libcom.org/library/marxism-prefigurative-communism-problem-workers-control-carl-boggs. Accessed May 28, 2020.
26 Albert Meltzer, *I Couldn't Paint Golden Angels* (Edinburgh: AK Press, 1996), 322.

personal ethics, meso-level *organizational modeling*, macro-level *political agitation*, or in some combination of these locations. It is precisely its location in the very "sensuousness" of our continuously unfolding lived experience, private and communal, that makes anarchism such a compelling and imperative proposition. Having said that, in the examples I offer at the end of this text emphasis is placed on the meso-level of activity. This decision is based on certain beliefs I hold concerning "what is possible," on how I think my model reader will most likely and effectively apply these ideas, and, finally, on my own life experience.

ORDER

When Pierre-Joseph Proudhon (1809–1865) proclaimed himself an anarchist by writing "I am (in the full force of the term) an anarchist"—apparently the first person ever to do so *with enthusiasm*—he prefaced it with an equally provocative statement: "Although a firm friend of order."[27] The subtle implication is that all the other forms of governance that his interlocutor assumed him to be advocating—republicanism, democracy, constitutionalism, aristocracy—invariably lead to the chaotic and violent outcomes of which anarchism was, and still is, accused. It should not require more than a moment's reflection

---

27 *What is Property*, 272. A similarly provocative motto: "As man seeks justice in equality, so society seeks order in anarchy" (chapter 5, part 2). "Anarchy is order" is another such motto, often attributed to Proudhon but apparently apocryphal. See Shawn Wilbur, "Anarchy is Order (Wait! What?) *The Libertarian Labyrinth*, https://www.libertarian-labyrinth.org/contrun/anarchy-is-order-wait-what. Accessed May 31, 2020. Until Proudhon's utterance, and since 1539 in English, the term "anarchy" was used exclusively in the derogatory sense of "a state of lawlessness" and "political disorder." The *Oxford English Dictionary* entry reads: "1539. R. Taverner tr. Erasmus *Prouerbes* (1552) 43: This unleful lyberty or lycence of the multytude is called an Anarchie." The first English attestation of "anarchist," as, namely, "one who upsets settled order," is: 1678 R. Cudworth *True Intellect. Syst. Universe* i. iv. 319: "That the Egyptians were universally Atheists and Anarchists, such as...resolved all into Senseless Matter as the first and highest Principle."

for the reader to become convinced that Proudhon was correct in his sly implication. Let your imagination glide over the past one hundred years. Behold the incessant warfare (some thirty-six conflicts, killing over a quarter of a billion people and counting), genocides (ten and counting, killing over twenty million people and counting), and financial meltdowns (some thirty-one, costing taxpayers trillions of dollars in corporate bailouts). How do we even begin to calculate the destabilization, destruction, and death happening under the auspices of our ostensibly orderly systems of governance? Forget a hundred years. In a single year, air pollution alone kills over seven million people. In the span of a couple of months in Europe alone a recent industrialization-exacerbated heat wave was responsible for more than 70,000 deaths. In Europe! In a single day alone the mass destruction of animals for human consumption amounts to some *two billion*—in a single day! Every two *seconds*, someone is forcibly displaced from his or her home due to violent conflict or persecution, adding up to nearly 80 million refugees altogether.[28] Let's consider something as fundamental to life on this planet as water. According to the World Health Organization, three quarters of a billion people "lack even a basic drinking-water service, including 144 million people who are dependent on surface water." At least two billion people "use a drinking water source contaminated with faeces," contributing to nearly a million deaths from diarrhea every year, a third of them children under the age of five, all 1,000,000 of them wholly preventable. Surely, world governments are improving the situation, right? No. In a mere five years, the WHO estimates, *half of the world's population* will be exposed to such water devastating conditions. When we input the numbers for other life essentials, such as food and shelter, this disaster is exacerbated exponentially. And let's be clear: the disaster is not limited to "the developing world." The disorder wrought by our current systems of government is global. If you live in places like California and Colorado,

28 The United Nations Refugee Agency, https://www.unhcr.org/en-us/figures-at-a-glance.html. Accessed June 1, 2020.

you and your loved ones are facing that looming water catastrophe no less than people in Cambodia and Cameroon.[29]

It would obviously be too much to attempt a thorough analysis of the relationship between such destruction and the intertwined global system of capitalist governments and economics (including the state capitalism of "communist" China). My purpose here is, rather, to stimulate you toward your own investigation and conclusions. I feel confident that you will find yourself winding down an eye-opening path. Consider, for instance, these two headlines from mainstream news on May 23, 2020: "Brazil minister calls for environmental deregulation while public distracted by COVID" (Reuters);[30] and "American billionaires got $434 billion richer during the pandemic" (CNBC).[31] We don't have to be cynics or conspiracy theorists to consider the possibility that "Under capitalism, everything is a business opportunity—catastrophes, from tsunamis to wars, are no exception."[32] Sadly, there is an abundance of evidence that not only bears out this premise, but

29 On warfare and its death toll: https://www.britannica.com/topic/list-of-wars-2031197;https://en.wikipedia.org/wiki/List_of_wars_by_death_toll;On genocides: https://ourworldindata.org/genocides; On financial crises: https://www.caproasia.com/2016/04/12/economic-crisis-since-1900-2015;https://projects.propublica.org/bailout/; On animal deaths: https://sentientmedia.org/how-many-animals-are-killed-for-food-every-day; On air pollution and climate-related deaths: https://www.who.int/health-topics/air-pollution#tab=tab_1;https://www.who.int/news-room/fact-sheets/detail/climate-change-and-health; On drinking water: https://www.who.int/news-room/fact-sheets/detail/drinking-water. Accessed May 24, 2020.

30 Reuters, https://www.reuters.com/article/us-brazil-politics-environment/brazil-minister-calls-for-environmental-deregulation-while-public-distracted-by-covid-idUSKBN22Y30Y. Accessed May 23, 2020.

31 CNBC, https://www.cnbc.com/2020/05/21/american-billionaires-got-434-billion-richer-during-the-pandemic.html?. Accessed May 23, 2020. As if that weren't bad enough, that is juxtaposed to a *Fortune* headline in my feed: "38.6 million have filed for unemployment during the pandemic—greater than the combined population of 21 states." https://fortune.com/2020/05/21/us-unemployment-rate-numbers-claims-this-week-total-job-losses-may-21-2020-benefits-claims-job-losses. Accessed May 23, 2020.

32 Jake Johnson, "If Nature is Sacred, Capitalism is Wicked," *Commondreams*, https://www.commondreams.org/views/2016/10/03/if-nature-sacred-capitalism-wicked. Accessed May 23, 2020.

suggests that we must take it much further.[33] Doing so will require that we suspend our belief that the never-ending catastrophes that define our world—environmental collapse, endless warfare, widespread hunger, obscene financial inequality, racial and gender oppression, and so on—are the result of fixable glitches in an otherwise stable system or of incompetent, temporary leadership. The additional step is to consider a deeply disturbing possibility: *disorder is an integral feature of the system*; the aim of the neoliberal capitalist system under which we live is precisely *to exacerbate disorder*.

> An economic system that requires constant growth...generates a steady stream of disasters all on its own, whether military, ecological or financial. The appetite for easy, short-term profits offered by purely speculative investment has turned the stock, currency, and real estate markets into crisis-creation machines.[34]

Naomi Klein calls such a system—namely, our global system—"disaster capitalism." She uses this, and its adjunct term "shock doctrine," to describe "the brutal tactic of using the public's disorientation following a collective shock—wars, coups, terrorist attacks, market crashes or natural disasters—to push through radical pro-corporate measures."[35] We don't have to agree with Klein's contention that the shock doctrine is a direct and intentional result of free market economic theories developed at the University of Chicago beginning in the 1950s.[36] My

---

33 Start with, for instance, Naomi Klein, *The Shock Doctrine: The Rise of Disaster Capitalism* (New York: Picador Press, 2008) and David Graeber, *Debt: The First Thousand Years* (New York: Melville Press, 2011).

34 Klein, *The Shock Doctrine*, 426.

35 Naomi Klein, "How Power Profits from Disaster," *The Guardian*, https://www.theguardian.com/us-news/2017/jul/06/naomi-klein-how-power-profits-from-disaster. Accessed May 23, 2020.

36 The Chicago school rejuvenated classical theories of economic liberalism. (Hence, the term "neoliberalism.") The classical term *laissez-faire*, letting-be, captures the general economic strategy of this system: deregulation, privatization, globalization of markets, free trade, competition.

purpose here is to sow in your mind the seed of suspicion that whatever other purposes our current "world order" may serve, *order* is not one of them, or at least not order in the sense of minimizing chaos, reducing suffering, and universally maximizing potential for wellbeing. And it is for the promotion of order in this latter sense that everyone from Proudhon forward has declared themselves anarchist.

My logical next step would be to present you with anarchist theoretical solutions for creating order and, even more usefully, to give practical examples. Sociologist Beth Hartung, for instance, insists that "instances of anarchistic social order must complete the argument. Accusations of idealism can only be countered with historical examples; criticisms concerning a lack of rigor, with theoretical synthesis."[37] Given the abundance of both theoretical and practical material in the anarchist archive, this move is not difficult to make. For instance, I could outline the minute instructions presented in Peter Kropotkin's (1842–1921) classic *The Conquest of Bread* or Murray Bookchin's more recent *Libertarian Municipalism*. In such works you will find detailed advice on how to proceed in an anarchist society concerning, for instance, the formation of the family; the procuring of food, clothing, and shelter; the management of leisure time; the structure of work; the use of money; the management and maintenance of big industry, agriculture, energy, infrastructure, banking, and technology; the confederation of towns and cities; criminal justice and the management of deviancy; municipalization of the economy; stewardship of the ecosystem, and way, way beyond. If you find value in such an approach, or perhaps are curious, by all means scour the archive.[38] I would, however, advise against placing too much stock in that approach. I have several reasons for doing so. First, I suspect that you will find such works unbearably tedious, somewhat like that list itself. Planner-theorists must, in their effort to create sound solutions, of necessity provide an abundance of

37 Beth Hartung, "Anarchism and the Problem of Order," *Mid-American Review of Sociology*, 1983, Vol. VIII, No. 1:84.

38 I recommend beginning at the searchable *Anarchist Library*, https://theanarchistlibrary.org/special/index. Accessed May 23, 2020.

detail, anticipate objections, counter those objections with more details and carefully-considered caveats, and so on and so forth. Such work is, of course, valuable for stimulating our imaginations, for revealing the role of historical contingency in fashioning our present, and for shifting our perspectives concerning what is possible. But if you are reading with a skeptical attitude—as I assume and indeed encourage—I just don't see how you will ever see through the mass of detail to something like a clarifying "solution." Storm clouds of objections gather quickly around every detail.

Awaiting us just beyond the cloud-mass of tediousness is that of relevance. Anarchism, in fact, offers us numerous instances of *actualizing* its plan for a new society. It does so in terms of both the historical past and the contemporary present. I would love to tell you about the extraordinary achievement of anarchists in Spain between 1936 and 1939. After witnessing U.S. president Donald Trump threaten to unleash the American military on the "professional anarchists" and "antifa" (anti-fascists) responsible for the "acts of domestic terror" during demonstrations against the police murder of George Floyd in Minneapolis,[39] I am sure you would be heartened by the Spanish anarchists' ferocious fight against the gathering forces of fascism in their own day. How impressed you would be to learn that, organized in trade unions and community centers numbering some one million members, anarchists controlled the economy in Catalonia and Valencia, in the industrialized northeast region of Spain.[40] With extraordinary

---

39 See *The Washington Post*, "Trump's threat to send in troops just got more ugly and dangerous," https://www.washingtonpost.com/opinions/2020/06/02/trumps-threat-send-troops-just-got-more-ugly-dangerous. Accessed June 4, 2020. On "antifa," see footnote 67.

40 See Stuart Christie, *We, the Anarchists! A study of the Iberian Anarchist Federation (FAI) 1927-1937* (Oakland: AK Press, 2008); and "The Spanish Civil War: Anarchism in Action, *Black Rose Anarchist Federation*, https://blackrosefed.org/spain-anarchism-in-action. Accessed June 4, 2020. Christie was imprisoned in 1964 while smuggling explosives as part of a plot to assassinate the Spanish right-wing military dictator, Francisco Franco. See Christie's memoir, *Granny Made Me an Anarchist: General Franco, The Angry Brigade and Me* (Oakland: AK Press, 2007).

efficiency they managed heavy industry, kept the railways and public transit systems running, oversaw the thriving manufacturing and retail sectors, and successfully socialized the agriculture, health care, and entertainment industries. In opposition to the repressive patriarchal policies of the Catholic Church, they provided universal childcare services, legalized abortion, and implemented gender-equal pay. Thirty-year-old George Orwell left us this firsthand account in *Homage to Catalonia*:

> Waiters and shop-walkers looked you in the face and treated you as an equal. Servile and even ceremonial forms of speech had temporarily disappeared. Nobody said "Senior" or "Don" or even "Usted;" everyone called everyone else "Comrade" and "Thou," and said "Salud!" instead of "Buenos dias"...There was no unemployment, and the price of living was still extremely low; you saw very few conspicuously destitute people, and no beggars except the gypsies. Above all, there was a belief in the revolution and the future, a feeling of having suddenly emerged into an era of equality and freedom. Human beings were trying to behave as human beings and not as cogs in the capitalist machine.

We all know that the author of *Animal Farm* is not a starry-eyed utopian. Orwell readily relates the anarchists' many failures:

> The town had a gaunt untidy look, roads and buildings were in poor repair, the streets at night were dimly lit for fear of air-raids, the shops were mostly shabby and half-empty. Meat was scarce and milk practically unobtainable, there was a shortage of coal, sugar, and petrol, and a really serious shortage of bread. Even at this period the bread-queues were often hundreds of yards long.

As a balanced reporter, Orwell is careful to mention that all of this, good and bad, was happening in the "evil atmosphere of war." And, "Yet, so far as one could judge," despite warfare and deprivation, "the people were contented and hopeful."[41]

Yes, I would love to wax eloquent about this extraordinary display of anarchism in action. It would render moot the endless accusation of anarchist "impracticality." You would behold the massive mainstream popularity of anarchism in a not too distant past. You would behold anarchism offering hope to the people, and recommending practical solutions in all facets of their daily lives. You would witness anarchism largely delivering on its promise. You would also witness the brutal forces that have led to anarchists' defeat time and time again. You would behold the betrayals and power-grabs of the communists and republicans on the left, and the murderous assaults by the conservatives, nationalists, fascists, and Nazis on the right. I think that, by the end, you would fully understand that in 1939 mass organized anarchism disappeared from the face of the earth.

As intriguing as this real-life "success" story of anarchist order would be, I doubt it would contribute much toward convincing you of the value of anarchism for your own life. Around every instance of success gather clouds of irrelevancy. 1930s Spain is worlds away from 2020s America, right? But does the same go for a contemporary example, one unfolding *on this very day*? I am referring to Rojava, a region in northeastern Syria that declared its autonomy in 2012. Significantly, for our purposes, Rojava has ordered itself along anarcha-feminist principles.[42] According to a recent report of the Anarchist Federation, many anarchists support the Rojava revolution, "a near-anarchist catalyst for social revolution in the region...similar to the revolutionary situation in Spain in 1936."[43] Why would they do so? For one thing,

41 All George Orwell quotes from *Homage to Catalonia*, published in 1938, searchable at *The Anarchist Library*, https://theanarchistlibrary.org/library/george-orwell-homage-to-catalonia. Accessed June 4, 2020.

42 It is officially known as the Autonomous Administration of North and East Syria. It autonomous status is *de facto* only.

43 "Anarchist Federation Statement on Rojava." As the less than full endorsement

Rojava's system of governance is decentralized, non-hierarchical, and egalitarian. Power is distributed throughout a population of over four million ethnically and linguistically diverse people living in seven distinct regions, hundreds of distinct neighborhoods, and several thousand communes. "Distributed power" is an anarchist ideal. It means governance without a state, wherein those distinct areas exercise autonomy in governing themselves. In other words, in contrast to the nation-state "democracies" of the West, in Rojava the motto that "Anarchism is democracy taken seriously" comes to life. Order is maintained not through coercive laws and the constant threat of state punishment (e.g., fines, police intervention, prison, etc.), but through the actual empowerment of citizens to participate directly in the decisions affecting their lives. In short, anarchists support Rojava because it is "a precious experiment in direct democracy," as *The New York Times* (of all sources) reports from the field, where "a new form of self-government is being built from the ground up." That statement is from former British diplomat, Carne Ross, whose intimate, close-range participation in the western democratic process, he says, destroyed his trust in the nation-state governance. His participation in the Rojava democracy, by contrast, turned him into "an accidental anarchist." What so impressed him was the robust decision-making process of self-governance at the local level. He witnessed everywhere a lack of hierarchy, even in the military. He witnessed the equality of women, who, even though coming of age in the brutally patriarchal society of the past, were as likely as any man to speak up, agitate, and lead. All of this, he says, was "confusing: I kept looking for a hierarchy, the singular leader, or signs of a government line, when, in fact, there was none; there were just groups."[44] Zelal Ceger, co-chairwoman of

---

of "near-anarchist" suggests, this report is mostly skeptical of the anarchist *bona fides* of Rojava. https://libcom.org/news/anarchist-federation-statement-rojava-december-2014-02122014. Accessed June 8, 2020.

44 Carne Ross, "The Kurds' Democratic Experiment," *New York Times*, https://www.nytimes.com/2015/09/30/opinion/the-kurds-democratic-experiment.html. Accessed June 8, 2020. Ross wrote the script for the movie "Accidental Anarchist:" http://www.

the Movement for a Democratic Society in Rojava, explains:

> Our system is not like that in Europe. For example, go to our villages and look. If a house gets damaged, the whole village fixes that house together. The natural society was created in Mesopotamia, and even now we still have some of that with us, it's our basis. As such, our people are ready to create a communal life. But in the last 2,000 years of life under the state system, the state wanted to remove the communal life and ruin it for the people, and wanted society to disperse. After the [democratic and feminist] revolution started, we're coming together once again to build up that life.[45]

Ceger's reference to "communal life" illuminates three points crucial to our discussion on order. It will be instructive to explore them further. The first point is that the Rojavan mode of governance was catalyzed by ideas developed by anarchist theorist Murray Bookchin.[46] These ideas where implemented in Rojava on the recommendation of the Kurdish political leader, Abdullah Öcalan. Öcalan became acquainted with Bookchin's theory of "communalism" in the Turkish island prison where he is currently serving a life sentence for armed insurrection. In fact, Öcalan considers himself Bookchin's "student," and "through his lawyers, began recommending [Bookchin's books] *Urbanization Without Cities* to all mayors in Turkish Kurdistan and *Ecology of Freedom* to all militants."[47]

---

accidentalanarchist.net.

45 "Rojava: The radical eco-anarchist experiment betrayed by the West, and bludgeoned by Turkey," *Infoshop News*, http://news.infoshop.org/middle-east/rojava-the-radical-eco-anarchist-experiment-betrayed-by-the-west-and-bludgeoned-by-turkey. Accessed June 8, 2020.

46 See Bookchin's pamphlet, *Communalism: A Liberatory Alternative*, https://www.communalismpamphlet.net/index.html#introduction. Accessed June 9, 2020.

47 See Janet Biehl, "Bookchin, Öcalan, and the Dialectics of Democracy," *New Compass: Toward an Ecological Society*, http://new-compass.net/articles/bookchin-%C3%B6calan-and-dialectics-democracy. Accessed June 9, 2020.

The second point is that, as much as Bookchin's influence is felt, this form of non-state, federated, direct democracy, whether labeled communalism or anarchism or anything else, is in essence *ancient*—in Rojava's case, "created in Mesopotamia" (ca. 3100–539 B.C.E.). This notion that its origin lies deep within humanity's past is, in any case, a common rhetorical trope in anarchist literature. Peter Kroptokin first expressed this view in 1910 when, in his seminal article for the *Encyclopedia Britannica*, he claimed that stateless societies founded on voluntary agreements between autonomous communities "have always existed in mankind, in opposition to the governing hierarchic conception and tendency."[48] More recently, Peter Marshall, in his monumental history of anarchism, aptly titled *Demanding the Impossible*, continues in this rhetorical vein. Anarchism, he writes, is a form of order that first appeared with the earliest "moral protest against oppression and injustice:"

> The very first human societies saw a constant struggle between those who wanted to rule and those who refused to be ruled or to rule in turn. The first anarchist was the first person who felt the oppression of another and rebelled against it. He or she not only asserted the right to think independently but challenged authority, whatsoever form it took. As a recognizable trend in human history, the thread of anarchism, in thought and deed, may be traced back several thousands of years. Anarchism began to take shape wherever people demanded to govern themselves in the face of power-seeking minorities...Throughout recorded history, the anarchist spirit can be seen emerging in the clan, tribe, village community, independent city, guild and union.[49]

48 Peter Kropotkin, *Anarchism*, https://theanarchistlibrary.org/library/petr-kropotkin-anarchism-from-the-encyclopaedia-britannica. Accessed June 8, 2020.
49 Peter Marshall, *Demanding the Impossible* (Oakland: PM Press, 1991), 12.

The "anarchist sensibility," so understood, thus possessed Daoists in ancient China, Buddhists in sixth century B.C.E. India, Greeks in the days of Socrates, revolutionary Christian mystics and millenarians of the Middle Ages, English dissenters known as the Diggers and the Ranters in the seventeenth century, common citizens in the town halls of colonial New England, and beyond. Without question, we are wading into some murky anachronism here. So, let's slow down. The notion of a culture-free, universal anarchist spirit or sensibility cries out for further analysis. Surely, a *direct* correspondence between classical anarchism and these various modes of "communalism" cannot withstand historical and conceptual scrutiny. Yet, the work of anthropologists and historians does raise the plausibility of the prior presence of what would in the nineteenth century be described as nominally "anarchist" principles and values.

> There are countless historical precedents that model communalism's institutional and ethical principles. Small-scale and tribal-based communities provide many such examples. In North America, the Six Nations Haudenasanee (Iroquois) Confederacy governed the region east of the Great Lakes by confederal direct democracy for over 800 years. In coastal Panama, the Kuna continue to manage an economically vibrant island archipelago. Prior to the devastation of colonization and slavery, the Igbo of the Niger Delta practiced a highly cosmopolitan form of communal management. More recently, in Chiapas, Mexico, the Zapatista Movement have reinvented pre-Columbian assembly politics through hundreds of autonomous *municipios* and five regional capitals called *caracoles* (snails) whose spirals symbolize the joining of villages.[50]

50 Eleanor Finley, "Reason, Creativity and Freedom: The Communalist Model," https://theanarchistlibrary.org/library/eleanor-finley-reason-creativity-and-freedom-the-communalist-model. Accessed June 15, 2020. See also: David Graeber, *Fragments of an Anarchist Anthropology* (Chicago: Prickly Paradigm Press, 2004); Harold Barclay,

Such examples of vibrant non-capitalist, non-state, communalist societies are extremely valuable for several reasons. They help us to imagine possibilities beyond our current constructions, they remind us that the current status quo is not inevitable and eternal, and they offer us concrete strategies for action. As enticing as such a line of exploration is, however, I fear that such an ahistorical approach will fail to convince you. Even if you are impressed by these examples, you may nonetheless find it impossible to establish their relevance and adaptability to our own time and place. If you are indeed taking that position, you are in harmony with a certain anarchist sensibility that insists that we must begin our deliberations on a transformed society *here and now*. An ahistorical approach runs counter to that sensibility.

More serious problems accompany the third point, namely, that this ancient mode of governance is "natural." Ceger may well be alluding to Rojava's commitment to ecological sustainability. This commitment is derived from Bookchin's concept of the "organic society," renamed by Öcalan as the "natural society." In natural society, he contends, people lived "as part of nature," and "human communities were part of the natural ecology."[51] In both Bookchin's and Öcalan's accounts, the "naturalness" of living in ecological balance was destroyed with the rise of human-imposed hierarchy, which had as a consequence the domination over nature: "Instead of being a part of nature," hierarchic society viewed "nature increasingly as a resource."[52] At work here is a "fundamental assumption of anarchism," namely, that "nature flourishes best if left to itself."[53] Crucially, moreover, "The same might be said of human beings."[54] That is, a belief in the *general* "naturalness" of its

---

People without Government: An Anthropology of Anarchy; Brian Morris, "Anthropology and Anarchism: Learning from Stateless Societies, https://archive.org/details/AnarchyAJournalOfDesireArmedNoOne/page/n11. Accessed June 15, 2020.

51 Biehl, "Bookchin, Öcalan."

52 Biehl, "Bookchin, Öcalan."

53 Marshall, *Demanding*, 21.

54 Marshall, *Demanding*, 21.

principles, beyond its ecological specificity, is another common trope in anarchism's self-understanding.

> It is interfering, dominating rulers who upset the natural harmony and balance of things. It is only when they try to work against the grain, to block the natural flow of energy, that trouble emerges in society. The anarchist confidence in the advantages of freedom, of letting alone, is thus grounded in a kind of cosmic optimism. Without the interference of human beings, natural laws will ensure that spontaneous order will emerge.[55]

Classically, Mikhail Bakunin (1814–1876) stated this in dialectical terms: "the harmony of natural forces appears only as the result of a continual struggle, which is the real condition of life and of movement. In nature, as in society as well, order without struggle is death."[56] Since the present text is a manifesto and not a theoretical work, I want only to suggest that this notion of a "natural order" is as dangerous as it is dubious. Consider, for instance that the very "disaster capitalism" that contemporary anarchism is so bent on undoing is founded on this exact same principle. In his 1776 classic of free-market capitalism, *The Wealth of Nations*, Adam Smith argued that trade markets are governed by an "invisible hand," a mysterious force that somehow knows better than any actual living human agent what is good for the whole of society, and is thus best left alone.[57]

> Every individual...is led by an invisible hand to promote an end which was no part of his intention. Nor is it always the worse for the society that it was no part of. By pursuing his own interest he frequently promotes that of the society more effectually than when he really intends to promote it.

55 Marshall, *Demanding*, 21.

56 Marshall, *Demanding*, 22.

57 Adam Smith, *Wealth of Nations* (Oxford : Oxford University Press , [1776] 1998), 291-292.

Smith's invisible hand metaphor has become linked to the *laissez-faire* ("let-do") model of governing, whereby government intervention in "the market" is drastically limited precisely in order to permit the invisible hand naturally to work its magic. In today's neoliberal world, it is arguably this "free market," more so than government, that is the dominant ordering mechanism of society. My point is that not only do I *not* wish to persuade you with this rhetoric of anarchism's "naturalness," but positively encourage you to reject it. Even if we could prove that anarchist values are "innate" or "natural," where would we be? Right where we are! That is, we would still have the task of changing the material structures within which any value or disposition is either engendered or impeded. Having said that, the conceits of universality and naturalness do suggest a line of argument that, I feel, will go some way toward persuading you of anarchism's value.

This line of argument was on display in the opening of this manifesto. In a short text titled *Are You an Anarchist? The Answer May Surprise You!*, anthropologist David Graeber (1961–2020) takes the same tack of posing a question, asking the reader to determine where he or she stands on it, and then pointing out that a negative or an affirmative answer, by turns, implicates the reader in an anarchist mode of being. To return to one of our first questions: "If there's a line to get on a crowded bus, do you wait your turn and refrain from elbowing your way past others even in the absence of police?" If you answer yes, you are acting out of a principle of order that is definitive of an anarchist: self-organization. If, in such situations, a person acts in an orderly manner *not* because of some threat of penalty or public reprobation, but because it is the best way to accomplish the task at hand—getting oneself and others on the bus!—than that person is being driven by an explicitly anarchist value. Is this too trivial an example? Well, consider the fact that throughout the world, with every ticking second of every day, virtually all of humanity is operating under a self-imposed ordering rule of cooperative self-organization. From friend-group relations, to driving in rush hour traffic, to grocery shopping, to large crowd participation such as concert-going, even to mass street demonstrations, we humans exhibit a remarkable capacity for creating order and acting cooperatively, even where the conditions for chaos are rife. An anarchist assumption holds that where a shared need or interest exist, people are capable of coming together and, through a combination of prior experience and improvised experimentation, of creating the mode of organization required to accomplish their aim. The assumption further holds that not only does this result require neither an external authority, a top-down leadership mechanism, nor a threat of punishment, but that it positively depends on *their absence*. This anti-authoritarian/anti-coercion element may strike readers as implausible. But imagine such an external force, say a police officer, exerting its authority on our cooperative bus line. What end could that possibly serve?

We do not need to go as far as advocating "universality" and "naturalness" to be persuaded by such a line of argument. The crucial claim merely revolves around *capacity*. If you accept the premise that those people standing on the bus line have the capacity for self-organizing into an orderly group with a specific purpose to achieve, why would any coercion be required? And if you can imagine it at such a minimal, everyday, level of life, why not extrapolate it out to larger, more complex, ones? Imagine this principle of self-organization applied in your family or friend groups, at your workplace, in the university where you study, in your town or city. Can you imagine the possibility that the members who comprise these configurations have the capacity *to figure things out together, for themselves*? Can you imagine that, furthermore, the very presence of an assertive authority—the strict parent, the controlling friend, the bossy boss, ordinance-bound township and city bureaucrats—stifles this capacity, suffocates creativity, and paralyzes progress?

At this point, a few questions naturally arise: won't the most aggressive people dominate everyone? what if someone dissents? how do we deal with disagreement? I can only recommend one guiding rule regarding such objections: anarchists welcome them. Such issues are already brewing beneath the surface anyway, so why not create an organizing process wherein they can come to expression and be dealt with? Have we not all witnessed for ourselves that authoritative, top-down leadership will not permit the necessary openness? Neither will fashioning a template in advance on how to deal with such inevitable difficulties. In any case, both approaches run counter to the anarchist principle of non-hierarchical, egalitarian, spontaneous self-organization.

Hopefully, I am making some progress in opening your eyes to the potential value of anarchism in your daily life. So, before we go further, now might be a good a time to address the two most damning, and persistent, criticisms of anarchism.

3.
Violence and Impracticality

How can we take anarchism seriously today? Most people hear the word and think "bombs" or "ridiculously impractical." The concept of anarchism elicits strong reactions. In my experience of discussing the topic with countless people since I attended an anarchism-inspired high school in the mid 1970s, those reactions fall into one of two extremes. One extreme is that anarchism names a violent maelstrom of social chaos. The other extreme is that anarchism names a puerile political philosophy that is ineffectual to the point of ridiculousness. We can put aside the somewhat quantum nature of this common bifurcation—like Schrodinger's cat, anarchism is a thing simultaneously alive and dead, simultaneously an excess of incendiary force and its utter lack—and consider whether these views have any merit. The short answer is, *yes, they have merit*: anarchism is as violent as it is feeble. Saying more about this answer will permit me to express the basic spirit and definition of anarchism as I am arguing for it in this text.

VIOLENCE

The main plank of anarchism is the removal of violence from human relations. —Errico Malatesta

Anarchism allows for a quite specific species of social violence. This species, however, is radically distinct from the variety assumed by liberals and conservatives alike. In the literal sense of the term, it is more accurate to designate this species as "counterviolence," or even, as Natasha Lennard puts it, "impossible nonviolence."[58] In the figurative sense that I mainly intend, the "violence" perpetuated by anarchism involves an adamant refusal to acquiesce to an unjust status quo, and a corresponding vehement insistence of constructing just ways of organizing social life. Anarchist violence is thus more an issue of responding to *violation* (of what it views as untenable norms, etc.) than it is of death and destruction. Given how large violence looms in discussions of anarchism, including, I assume, in many readers' imaginations, it will be best to wind our way slowly toward this conclusion.

The reader should view what follows as a kind of litmus test for determining where you stand on the issue of the necessity of forceful action in bringing about change. It is not, of course, intended to incite you to violence. Neither is it intended to corner you into sympathizing with violent perpetrators. In fact, such perpetrators represent a small minority within the anarchist tradition, past and present. Far more typical is the attitude expressed in the epigram, which alludes to the very incompatibility of destructive violence and the anarchist principles of non-coercion, non-domination, and good will camaraderie. Yet, given the extent to which the reception and reputation of anarchism has been marked by its relationship to violence, I feel it is best to address that relationship in all of its contradictory, deeply problematic messiness.

More, perhaps, than any other figure, Errico Malatesta embodied the tensions inherent in the story of this relationship. We heard from him earlier, fiercely advocating total revolution. Early in his life, he expressed the logic, and the justification, of anarchist violence as one of dire necessity.

> It is our aspiration and our aim that everyone should become socially conscious and effective; but to achieve

58 Natasha Lennard, *Being Numerous: Essays on the Non-Fascist Life* (London: Verso, 2019), 48.

> this end, it is necessary to provide all with the means of life and for development, and it is therefore necessary to destroy with violence, since one cannot do otherwise, the violence which denies these means to the workers.

The general position of first and second wave anarchists (i.e., from roughly 1840–1920) was that violence was part of the solution for those who advocated for justice and equality because the privileged minority would otherwise never give an inch. As an explicit strategy, however, violent tactics were eventually dismissed as ineffectual. Emma Goldman, Peter Kropotkin, and other major nineteenth century anarchist figures would eventually express views similar to Malatesta's passionate plea against violence in *Violence as a Social Factor*. Given the fact that anarchism has been so deeply branded, in the public's eye, as irredeemably violent, I cite Malatesta's mature view at length before giving the reader a fuller account.

> Violence, i.e., physical force, used to another's hurt, which is the most brutal form that struggle between men can assume, is eminently corrupting. It tends, by its very nature, to suffocate the best sentiments of man, and to develop all the antisocial qualities, ferocity, hatred, revenge, the spirit of domination and tyranny, contempt of the weak, servility towards the strong. And this harmful tendency arises also when violence is used for a good end...How many men who enter on a political struggle inspired with the love of humanity, of liberty, and of toleration, end by becoming cruel and inexorable proscribers...Anarchists who rebel against every sort of oppression and struggle for the integral liberty of each and who ought thus to shrink instinctively from all acts of violence which cease to be mere resistance to oppression and become oppressive in their turn are also liable to fall into the abyss of brutal force...The excitement caused by some recent explosions and the admiration for

> the courage with which the bomb-throwers faced death, suffices to cause many anarchists to forget their program, and to enter on a path which is the most absolute negation of all anarchist ideas and sentiments...In short it is our duty to call attention to the dangers attendant on the use of violence, to insist on the principle of the inviolability of human life, to combat the spirit of hatred and revenge, and to preach love and toleration.[59]

The Story of Anarchist Violence

The heyday of anarchist violence was roughly the mid-1870s to the early 1900s. This era is marked by a tactic called "propaganda by deed."[60] Like "propaganda by word" (an instance of which this manifesto aspires to be), propaganda by deed was seen as a "powerful means of awakening popular consciousness." Peter Kropotkin (1842–1921), an early advocate and later renouncer of this tactic, believed that particular acts of violence had a catalyzing capacity to "awaken boldness and the spirit of revolt by preaching by example."[61] The "awakening" alluded to by Kropotkin involves critical awareness of the social, political, and economic forces held by the emerging socialist analyses to be at work in our collective oppression, as well as the capacity of each individual to strike against those forces.[62] The "example" being demon-

---

59 Errico Malatesta, *Violence as a Social Factor*, n.p., https://theanarchistlibrary.org/library/errico-malatesta-violence-as-a-social-factor. Accessed November 5, 2020.

60 The term "propaganda" now has the purely pejorative connotations of "biased," manipulative," misleading," and so on. In nineteenth-century usage it was a neutral term. It simply meant what its root word, Latin *propagare*, denoted: *to propagate, to spread.*

61 Olivier Hubac-Occhipinti, "Anarchist Terrorists of the Nineteenth Century," In *The History of Terrorism: From Antiquity to ISIS*, ed. Chaliand Gérard and Blin Arnaud (Oakland, California: University of California Press, 2016), 116. Writing in the Swiss socialist journal *Le Révolté*, Kropotkin would eventually conclude that "a structure based on centuries of history cannot be destroyed with a few kilos of dynamite." See James H. Billington, *Fire in the Minds of Men: Origins of the Revolutionary Faith* (New Jersey: Transaction Books, 1998), 417.

62 From its explicit inception with Pierre-Joseph Proudhon (1809–1865), who

strated in propaganda by deed concerns the necessarily transgressive manifestation of individual or collective autonomous power.[63] So, to whatever extent a person might be convinced *in theory* of the value of anarchism as an analysis of the structural causes of social suffering, it is only through immediate *assaults* on either the individual or collective perpetrators of those structures, this thinking goes, that meaningful change can come about.[64] For reasons that make sense within the late nineteenth-century context of the tactic, the gathering of activists agitating for working people globally, called the International Anarchists Conference, boldly declared in London on July 14, 1881 that "the time has come to…act, and to add propaganda by deed and insurrectionary actions to oral and written propaganda, which have proven ineffective."[65] Ineffective toward what end? Toward, of course, the destruction of oppressive structures. Propaganda by deed aimed to add ballast to the spoken and written word. It did so by placing "the dagger, the rifle, and dynamite" in the anarchist's arsenal of propagation.[66]

---

provocatively declared in *What is Property* (1840), "I am an anarchist," anarchism was considered a variety of socialism. It still is, although, ever since the split between the Marx and Bakunin factions at the fifth congress of the International Workingmen's Association in 1872, typically with the modification "libertarian" in distinction to "authoritarian." For a full account, see, Ann Robertson, *The Philosophical Roots of the Marx-Bakunin Conflict,* https://www.marxists.org/reference/archive/bakunin/bio/robertson-ann.htm. Accessed November 5, 2020. The core concept of socialism is simple: public, rather than individual or corporate, ownership of the "means" (machinery, equipment, raw materials, facilities, etc.), production, and distribution of social wealth.

63 Necessarily transgressive, because "Everything is good for us which falls outside legality." (Kropotkin in *Le Révolté*, December 1880, quoted in Jean Maitron, *Histoire du mouvement anarchiste en France (1880-1914)* (Paris: Société universitaire d'éditions et de librairie, 1951), 70.

64 A "structure" is a socially established arrangement of complex parts, the purpose of which is to catalyze specific activities and to disable others. For example, the life of a university student *as* university student, like the careers of professors, administrators, and staff, is determined to a decisive degree by requirements, rules and regulations, customs, and so on, that largely float free of the people executing them. In this manner, students are *subjects of* the university because they are *subjected to*, and are, an anarchist would contend, *subjugated by*, the machinic structure that is the university.

65 Hubac-Occhipinti, "Anarchist Terrorists, 116.

66 Kropotkin in his Swiss journal, *Le Révolté*, in 1879. Cited by Miriam Brody,

As critics of anarchism rightly charge, the "deed" involved overt physical violence. But don't picture gangs of armed thugs roaming the streets, much less an organized discharge of militias or armies against the state. Observers of more recent anarchist violence may be tempted to picture the Molotov-throwing clashes of the German Autonomen against the police in Berlin in the 1970s and 1980s, or their most recent incarnation as the black bloc in 1999 during the anti-globalist "Battle of Seattle,"[67] or even the antifa (anti-fascist) interventions against neo-fascists and white supremacist in Charlottesville in 2017. These recent instances, which I will come back to later, are clearly the genetic offspring of the older generation of deed propagandists, but such contemporary large-scale demonstration tactics would not have worked for their purposes. Instead, they advocated the precise targeting of powerful individuals who were directly involved in the maintenance of the apparatus of oppression. Among the most prominent examples are the assassinations of members of the ruling class, such as King Umberto I of Italy, in 1900; Sadi Carnot, the president of the French Republic, in 1897; Empress Elizabeth of Austria in 1898, Antonio Canovas, the president of the Spanish Council of Ministers, in 1897; and of course President William McKinley of the United States, in 1901. (Gavrilo Princip, who assassinated Archduke Franz Ferdinand of Austria, committed his violence in the name of nationalism, not anarchism.)[68] Industry leaders were also targeted. A

"Introduction," in Emma Goldman, *Living my Life* (New York, Penguin, 2006 [1931]), xvii .

67 The current English terminology reveals the German heritage of these formations: antifa, from *antifaschistisch* (antifascist) and black bloc, from *Schwarze Block*, named for their black clothing and masks.

68 It is commonly believed that Gavrilo Princip (1894–1918), the assassin, was an anarchist. This is not accurate. Like countless other disaffected and searching youths of his day, Princip had indeed read the anarchists writers. At the *Gymnasium* in Sarajevo, he was exposed to, in his own words, "many anarchistic, socialistic, nationalistic pamphlets, belles letters and everything." As we read in "Dr. Martin Pappenheim's Conversations With Gavrilo Princip," ultimately, "Princip's radicalism became misdirected into the poison of nationalism and militarism." https://libcom.org/history/did-teenage-anarchists-trigger-world-war-one-what-was-politics-assassins-franz-ferdinand.

particularly notorious example is the attempted assassination of the American industrialist Henry Clay Frick, chairman of the Carnegie Steel Company, by Alexander Berkman (1870–1936), in 1892.[69] On at least one occasion—the bombing of Café Terminus in Paris, in 1894—the target was the class of people who owned and operated or otherwise acquired wealth from the factories and various emerging industries, and hence were deemed responsible for exploiting workers, namely, the "bourgeoisie."[70]

So, for the most part, the deed was carried out by a lone assailant targeting a specific person of influence. At least that was how the tactic was supposed to work. In one famous case—the 1906 bombing of the royal wedding procession of the Spanish king Alfonso XIII and his bride, Victoria Eugenie—twenty-four bystanders were killed and over a hundred wounded, but the king and his bride remained unharmed.[71] Remarkably, however, one historian estimates that throughout the several decades when propaganda by deed was practiced, "anarchists and anarchist sympathisers initiated perhaps 40 violent attacks...and were to blame for 100 deaths throughout the entire world."[72]

I hope you are surprised by these numbers, speculative as they may

---

Accessed November 5, 2020.

69 Although Berkman shot Frick twice in the neck and stabbed him with a dagger four times in the leg, the industrialist survived.

70 One person was killed and twenty were injured. For these and other cases of propaganda by deed, see Hubac-Occhipinti, "Anarchist Terrorists." Another valuable source is "Anarchist Incidents, 1886–1920: Topics in Chronicling America," at the Library of Congress's online *Research Guides*. Accessed May 1, 2020, https://guides.loc.gov/chronicling-america-anarchist-incidents. The somewhat outdated French term "bourgeoisie," originally referred to people who lived within the walled cities (*bourg*) as opposed to the nobility and to the peasants in the country. It eventually takes on the sense of a *class* of people, beginning, namely, with the merchants and the craftsmen who held political power, and then those who possess the bulk of social and financial capital.

71 Angel Smith *Anarchism, Revolution, and Reaction: Catalan Labour and the Crisis of the Spanish State, 1898-1923* (Oxford: Berghahn Books, 2007), 163.

72 Jeff Sparrow, "In the end, we forget the anarchists, bombers and 'lone wolves'. But the hysteria they provoke stays with us," *The Guardian*, accessed May 2, 2020, https://www.theguardian.com/commentisfree/2015/jan/02/in-the-end-we-forget-the-anarchists-bombers-and-lone-wolves-but-the-hysteria-they-provoke-stays-with-us.

be. I hope so only because of the corrective to a falsified historical record that such numbers serve. But by looking for surprise, I am not, of course, looking for your forgiveness of the killers. Writing in the heyday of propaganda by deed, Malatesta, furthermore, should disabuse us of any suggestion of a "they do it to" justification.

> Hatred and revenge seemed to have become the moral basis of Anarchism. "The bourgeoisie does as bad and worse." Such is the argument with which they tried to justify and exalt every brutal deed.[73]

Casting what is perhaps the greatest aspersion possible on a self-proclaimed anarchist ("authoritarian!"), Malatesta adds, "It is true that these ultra-authoritarians, who so strangely persist in calling themselves Anarchists, are but a small fraction who acquired a momentary importance owing to exceptional circumstances."[74]

Having said that, such low figures certainly raise questions: Why was the official reaction so vehemently hostile to anarchism? Why did the press of the day write headlines like "Cut Throats Caged," "Anarchist Leader and His Satanic Subalterns Jailed in Chicago," "The Cowardly Curs Quieted"?[75] Why did U.S. President Theodore Roosevelt, a self-declared "progressive," declare in 1908, "When compared with the suppression of anarchy, every other question sinks into insignificance"? Why were numerous draconian anti-socialist laws passed around the world? Most importantly for our purposes, why does this reputation persist down to the present day, even among intelligent, critically-aware people, as I imagine my readers to be?

One explanation is that the killing of a state official posed, or was perceived as posing, a legitimate threat to stability. After all, historians

73 Errico Malatesta, *Violence as a Social Factor*, n.p.

74 Errico Malatesta, *Violence as a Social Factor*, n.p.

75 *Omaha Daily Bee,* May 6, 1896. The latter two are actually subtitles of an article on "Chicago's Reign of Terror," which we now refer to as the Haymarket Affair/Riot/Massacre, depending on one's politics. Accessed May 1, 2020, https://chroniclingamerica.loc.gov/lccn/sn99021999/1886-05-06/ed-1/seq-1/#words=CUT+THROATS+CAGED

consider the assassination of Archduke Franz Ferdinand, heir apparent to the Austrian-Hungarian throne in 1917 to be a major contributor to World War I and the devastation that came in its wake. Yet other such destabilizing threats in that era—economic downturn, foreign hostilities, the advance of communism—do not appear to have elicited a similarly vehement response. My suggestion is that the "violent" threat of anarchism was, as I said at the outset, social in nature. As I will show in more detail later, anarchists were at the forefront of the justice movements of their day. Anarchist speakers, renowned for eloquent rhetorical skill, barnstormed the United States, speaking before hundreds and even thousands of receptive listeners. One of the most popular was Emma Goldman, whose "impassioned advocacy of politically unpopular ideas and causes like free love, anarchism, and atheism...led many of the powerful to fear and hate her." Famously, U.S. Attorney General Francis Caffey called her "a woman of great ability and of personal magnetism, and her persuasive powers make her an exceedingly dangerous woman." Perhaps the real threat of the anarchist orators lay in their relationship to the beleaguered masses as educators, "who in nationwide lecture tours spread modern ideas and practices to a young and provincial country."[76]

Returning to the harsh reality of propaganda by deed, I hope that exposing readers to an actual propagandist's justification behind the violence he committed will give perspective on this epoch of anarchist history. My purpose in doing so is to lay the groundwork for the reader's revised perception both of the true perpetrators of violence and of the actual version of violence that anarchism represents, then and now. We can do no better than listening to one Auguste Vaillant (1861–1894). In 1893, Vaillant, a committed anarchist, was arrested for throwing a bomb from the public gallery of the Palais-Bourbon in Paris into the Chamber of Deputies. Like countless others, Vaillant was anguished at his inability to support his wife and child on a

---

76 *The Emma Goldman Papers*, https://www.lib.berkeley.edu/goldman/MeetEmmaGoldman/index.html. Accessed November 5, 2020.

workingman's cruelly paltry wages. Vaillant was trapped inescapably in abject poverty with no way out. At his trial he confessed that he had contemplated suicide, but determined instead to die in a manner that meaningfully symbolized "the cry of a whole class that demands its rights and will soon add acts to words." (We hear in that statement that Vaillant shared Kropotkin's belief that propaganda by deed was a potent means of consciousness-raising and of "awakening boldness and the spirit of revolt.") Vaillant, at his trial, eloquently explained the general anarchist motivation for agitation, whether it applies to oneself or only to others:

> I have seen capital come, like a vampire, to suck the last drop of blood of the unfortunate pariahs. Then I came back [from an attempt to find work and dignity in Argentina] to France where it was reserved for me to see my family suffer atrociously. This was the last drop in the cup of my sorrow. Tired of leading this life of suffering and cowardice I carried this bomb to those who are primarily responsible for social misery.

Vallant's homemade nail bomb was so weak that only a few deputies were slightly injured. This meagre result, Vallant said, had been his intention from the outset. Still, he was, of course, quickly found guilty of attempted murder and sent to the guillotine.

> Gentleman, soon you will strike me. But in receiving your verdict, I will at least have the satisfaction of having wounded the existing society, this cursed society in which one may see a single man spending, uselessly, enough to feed thousands of families; an infamous society that permits a few individuals to monopolize social wealth.[77]

77 See, Hubac-Occhipinti, "Anarchist Terrorists, 127–128, and *The Anarchist Encyclopedia*. Accessed May 6, 2020, https://web.archive.org/web/20080123215947/http://recollectionbooks.com/bleed/Encyclopedia/VaillantAuguste.htm

We could consider many more instances of anarchist violence, real or imagined. Readers may be familiar with, for example, two such notorious American cases: the Haymarket Affair and the case of Sacco and Vanzetti.

The Haymarket Affair—variously referred to as the Haymarket Riot, Massacre, Episode, Incident, or Tragedy, depending, I suppose, on one's political leanings—is still considered both "an enduring symbol of the anarchist terror of that time,"[78] and *the* singular event that "influenced the history of labor in...the United States, and even the world...whose consequences are still being felt today."[79] On May 3, 1886, workers advocating for an eight-hour workday had gathered in Chicago's Haymarket Square. (I feel a need to repeat that with the proper emphasis: *advocating for an eight-hour workday!* The incendiary slogan of the day was: "Eight Hours for Work! Eight Hours for Rest! Eight Hours for What We Will!") This event was part of a coordinated national movement that commenced on May 1, 1886. Some 350,000–500,000 workers participated in a nationwide work stoppage. Their aim was simple: force the hands of employers and the government to adopt an eight-hour workday. The webisode, "The Rise of Labor," gives some context for this goal:

> Steelmen worked twelve hours a day, six days a week, for little pay. Textile workers—many of them children—worked sixty to eighty hours a week. Conditions were often dangerous. Miners worked underground with explosives but without safety regulations. In one year, 25,000 workers died on the job; many more were injured. Child workers had three times as many accidents as adults. If a person lost an arm in an accident, no one helped with doctor's bills. If a worker complained, he was fired. And women were often paid half a man's wages.[80]

---

78 Hubac-Occhipinti, "Anarchist Terrorists," 403.

79 "The Haymarket Affair," *Illinois Labor History Society*, http://www.illinoislaborhistory.org/the-haymarket-affair. Accessed July 17, 2020.

80 https://www.thirteen.org/wnet/historyofus/web09/segment6_p.html. Accessed July

It is this moment that gives birth to labor unions. The obvious purpose for unionization was the protection of workers and effective bargaining through strength in numbers. So, given that the Haymarket rally was a labor event, let's hear from one of its organizers, German immigrant August Spies (1855–1887), an upholsterer and a committed anarchist. Standing on the makeshift speaker's platform, Spies proclaimed:

> There seems to prevail the opinion in some quarters that this meeting has been called for the purpose of inaugurating a riot, hence these warlike preparations on the part of so-called "law and order." However, let me tell you at the beginning that this meeting has not been called for any such purpose. The object of this meeting is to explain the general situation of the eight-hour movement and to throw light upon various incidents in connection with it.

Tensions in Chicago were elevated. Two days before, Lucy Parsons led a peaceful march of some 35,000 workers down Michigan Avenue to high-spirited chants of "an eight-hour day/with no cut in pay!"[81] The next day, however, peace erupted into violence when the officers of "law and order" referred to by Spies, i.e., the Chicago police, attacked and killed picketing factory workers, predominantly Irish-Americans, at the McCormick Harvesting Machine Company plant. Perhaps it was fortuitous that this evening on Haymarket Square the expected turnout of 20,000 dwindled to a mere 200 or fewer. The event was quickly becoming anti-climactic. It began over an hour late. Most of the scheduled speakers did not show up. As darkness fell, a chilly wind kicked up,

---

17, 2020.

81 Parson's (1851–1942) was a remarkable woman. An African American, she was born enslaved. She later became a self-described anarcho-communist, and a leading figure in the labor struggle. Parsons became famous throughout the United States when she advocated for her white husband, Albert Parsons, who was implicated in, and eventually executed for, the Haymarket Affair. Read her speech, "I am an Anarchist," at *Black Past*, https://www.blackpast.org/african-american-history/1886-lucy-parsons-i-am-anarchist. Accessed July 17. 2020.

rain began to fall, and people began leaving. Even Chicago's pro-labor mayor, Carter Harrison, Sr., went home early.[82] Then, some 200 policemen appeared, marching shoulder to shoulder, clubs in hand, down the street and into the square. The captain bellowed at the speaker to stop and the crowd to disperse. Someone—to this day no one knows who it was—threw a bomb into the police ranks. The police began firing their pistols into the darkness and murky chaos. While the actual explosion killed one policeman, six others died later from gunshot wounds, and sixty were injured. Four workers were killed by gunshot, and numerous others injured. The crowd frantically fled the scene. In the subsequent investigation, one officer anonymously confessed to the *Chicago Tribune* that "A very large number of the police were wounded by each other's revolvers…It was every man for himself, and while some got two or three squares away, the rest emptied their revolvers, mainly into each other."[83] This anonymous statement gains credibility from an official report, which contains this account:

> [The police] swept both sidewalks with a hot and telling fire, and in a few minutes the Anarchists were flying in every direction. I then gave the order to cease firing, fearing that some of our men, in the darkness might fire into each other.[84]

Apparently, they did just that. Yet, eight anarchists were eventually convicted of conspiracy to murder, although neither the bomb thrower nor the source of the bomb were ever discovered. In fact, no evidence was presented at trial that tied any of the eight anarchists to the bomb in any way. In fact, some of them were not even present at Haymarket,

82 Bruce C. Nelson, *Beyond the Martyrs: A Social History of Chicago's Anarchists, 1870–1900* (New Brunswick: Rutgers University Press, 1988), 188.

83 Paul Avrich, *The Haymarket Tragedy* (Princeton: Princeton University Press, 1984), 209.

84 "Inspector John Bonfield report to Frederick Ebersold, General Superintendent of Police, 1886 May 30, *Chicago Historical Society*, http://www.chicagohistoryresources.org/hadc/manuscripts/m03/M03.htm#M03P020. Accessed July 17, 2020.

or in Chicago, that evening. Spies, our speaker, was one of four men eventually hanged. Standing on the gallows, shrouded, hands tied behind his back, Spies yelled out as the executioner placed the noose around his throat, "The day will come when our silence will be more powerful than the voices you strangle today!"[85]

Only a few years later, in 1893, John Peter Altgeld, the governor of Illinois, pardoned the three surviving Haymarket anarchists. As the legendary lawyer Clarence Darrow said at his funeral in 1902, Altgeld "fearlessly and knowingly bared his devoted head to the fiercest, most vindictive criticism ever heaped upon a public man, because he loved justice and dared to do the right." The right that Altgeld performed was "to redress one of the most shameful injustices in the state's history," the Haymarket trial.[86] It will be instructive to note the governor's reasons for taking the extraordinarily rare action of issuing a career-ending pardon to inconsequential workers:

> FIRST: That the jury which tried the case was a packed jury selected to convict.
>
> SECOND: That according to the law as laid down by the supreme court, both prior to and again since the trial of this case, the jurors, according to their own answers, were not competent jurors and the trial was therefore not a legal trial.
>
> THIRD: That the defendants were not proven to be guilty of the crime charged in the indictment.
>
> FOURTH: That as to the defendant Neebe, the state's attorney had declared at the close of the evidence that there was no case against him, and yet he has been kept in prison all these years.

---

85 Avrich, *Haymarket Tragedy*, 293.

86 "Governor John Peter Altgeld Pardons the Haymarket Prisoners," *Illinois Labor History Society*, http://www.illinoislaborhistory.org/labor-history-articles/governor-john-peter-altgeld-pardons-the-haymarket-prisoners. Accessed July 17, 2020.

> FIFTH: That the trial judge was either so prejudiced against the defendants, or else so determined to win the applause of a certain class in the community that he could not and did not grant a fair trial.[87]

The second notorious American case also ended in a governor's abashed pardon. This case, known as the Sacco and Vanzetti Affair, concerns Nicolo Sacco, a heel-trimmer by trade, and Bartolomeo Vanzetti, a fish peddler. In 1920, these two Italian immigrants, and self-professed anarchists, were accused of killing two employees during the anarchist-plot motivated robbery of a Braintree, Massachusetts factory. The details are not relevant to my purposes here.[88] What is relevant is that the shakiness of the evidence and the prevalence of blatant anti-Italian and anti-leftist sentiments in the case were so glaring that it became an international *cause célèbre*, with writers, academics, actors, religious leaders, and even future U.S. Supreme Court justice Felix Frankfurter, calling for a pardon when Sacco and Vanzetti were convicted. Instead, they were, of course, electrocuted. The only clear outcome of this "calamity," according to one prominent European observer, was that it laid bare "this frightful America, whose heart is made of stone; this America, for whom humanity does not exist."[89] Fifty years later, the governor of Massachusetts, Michael Dukakis, publicly admitting the tragic failure of the justice system to render

---

87 You can read this rare, extraordinarily courageous political pardon in its entirety, where each of these five points is exhaustively argued: "The Pardon of the Haymarket Prisoners (June 26, 1893)," *Famous Trials*, https://famous-trials.com/haymarket/1182-pardon. Accessed July 17, 2020.

88 For the details, see Moshik Temkin, *The Sacco and Vanzetti Affair: America on Trial* (New Haven: Yale University Press, 2009). The title of the book is, obviously, very telling in itself. The case of Sacco and Vanzetti was not a "trial" as much as an "affair," a controversial, convoluted, fiasco. It that regard, it had more in common with the 1894–1906 French political scandal, "L'Affaire Dreyfus," whereby an artillery captain was falsely accused of passing military secrets to the Germans. As with the identity of Sacco and Vanzetti as Italians and anarchists, a crucial key in understanding this affair is that fact that the accused, Albert Dreyfus, was Jewish, a merely tolerated outsider.

89 Temkin, *The Sacco and Vanzetti Affair*, 118.

a fair verdict to Sacco and Vanzetti, issued a proclamation that "any disgrace should be forever removed from their names."[90]

What might have instigated injustices so profoundly shameful that even agents of the state felt compelled to redress them? Since I am asking my reader to consider, however momentarily, violence from the side of anarchism, I will present the answer to this question from the perspective of labor. Today, labor, of course, stands nowhere near anarchism in either its self-understanding or articulation of values. In fact, on the political spectrum, labor is arguably closer to the center, where conservative meets liberal. Labor does, however, share at least one crucial premise with anarchism. And it is the reality behind this premise that provides the proper frame for anarchist—and labor—violence. Consider this explanation from the Illinois Labor History Society, under the entry "Governor John Peter Altgeld Pardons the Haymarket Prisoners:"

> Those enjoying increasingly concentrated wealth in Chicago had little patience with working people, especially those of foreign birth, who had the gall to stand up for their rights. Such activities were seen as a threat to the free market, the individual's right to work 10 to 12 hours a day for a pittance...The Chicago establishment, led by Joseph Medill's *Tribune*, saw the incident as a chance to wipe out the leadership of the city's radical labor movement and send a message to all who would seek just wages, decent working conditions, and reduced hours for working men and women.[91]

I could cite additional examples of violence. But it is not necessary. Whether you are prepared to believe that "The notorious events

90 See "Guide to the FBI Files on Sacco and Vanzetti on Microfilm," Cornell University Library website, https://tinyurl.com/y49ahlkv. Accessed July 17, 2020.

91 "Governor John Peter Altgeld Pardons the Haymarket Prisoners," *Illinois Labor History Society*, http://www.illinoislaborhistory.org/labor-history-articles/governor-john-peter-altgeld-pardons-the-haymarket-prisoners. Accessed July 17, 2020.

that took place in Chicago in 1886 [and elsewhere] had more to do with self-defense than terrorist action,"[92] as one scholar claims, I hope you will consider the outlines of a simple logic. Roughly, the logic goes like this: *Premise 1. Oppressed people—the poor, wage workers, and politically radical immigrants, in our examples—lack faith in "the system."* Experience has proven to them that the laws, with its courts and police; the politicians, with their massive government bureaucracy; and even the "respectable" class of citizens known, in the older parlance, as the bourgeoisie, or today simply as the middle class, with its investment in the perpetuation of the status quo and their privileged position within it, will block newcomers by all means necessary. *Premise 2. The means of oppression, exploitation, and denial of social goods can be summed up in a word: violence.* This premise holds that the very formations that make up the status quo, including, in addition to those just mentioned, the education system, the media, the entertainment industry, the corporate world, finance and banking, and so on, function in ways that cause widespread harm. The term for this variety of social harm is "structural violence:"

> Structural violence is one way of describing social arrangements that put individuals and populations in harm's way...The arrangements are structural because they are embedded in the political and economic organization of our social world; they are violent because they cause injury to people...Neither culture nor pure individual will is at fault; rather, historically given (and often economically driven) processes and forces conspire to constrain individual agency. Structural violence is visited upon all those whose social status denies them access to the fruits of scientific and social progress.[93]

---

92 Hubac-Occhipinti, "Anarchist Terrorists of the Nineteenth Century," 122. Speaking of self-defense, a headline from the *Washington Post* reads, "Trump ordered federal forces to quell Portland protests. But the chaos ended as soon as they left."

93 "Structural Violence," *Structural Violence: inequality and the harm it causes*, http://

Recall that "capitalist realism," as articulated by Mark Fisher, operates largely unobserved, like a "pervasive atmosphere," simultaneously conditioning and constraining perspectives, beliefs, and behaviors. I feel certain that few of my readers would characterize the American health care system as inherently "violent." But the claim here is that structural violence is typically invisible even to itself, even, that is, to the actual people who are subjected to the structure, both as agents and, literally, in this case, as patients.

> Over 20 years' worth of studies show that people of color who arrive at a hospital while having a heart attack are significantly less likely to receive aspirin, beta-blocking drugs, clot-dissolving drugs, acute cardiac catheterization, angioplasty, or bypass surgery. Race, class, and gender clearly make a difference in how patients are diagnosed and treated.[94]

Premise 2 holds, furthermore, that structural violence is enabled by a facade of naturalness and inevitably. That is, we have become so inured to "the way things are" that we fail to see that—like Ursula Le Guin's observation about the divine right of kings, which for millennia seemed as natural as the rising of the sun—our currently harmful social formations are wholly contingent human creations. What makes it so difficult to see this fact is that our shared social experience is saturated by features that legitimize the violence.

> Aspects of culture and social life—exemplified by religion, ideology, language, art, law and science—that can be used to justify or legitimise direct or structural violence, making

www.structuralviolence.org/structural-violence. Accessed July 19, 2020. The origination of this term is usually ascribed to Johan Galtung and his 1969 article "Violence, Peace, and Peace Research," *Journal of Peace Research*, Vol. 6, No. 3. (1969), 167–191. Galtung, a Norwegian sociologist, is considered a central figure in the founding of peace and conflict studies.

94 "Structural Violence," *Structural Violence: inequality and the harm it causes*, http://www.structuralviolence.org/structural-violence. Accessed July 19, 2020.

> direct and structural violence look, or even feel, right—or at least not wrong.[95]

We can take as an example the structure that, after health care, I imagine many people will find the least plausibly "violent." Virtually every instance of blackness and darkness—the angry black male "thug," the hyper-sexual black female, the black welfare queen, the negligent black father, etc.—proliferates through American culture as entertainment, whether on the internet, on television, in movies, in advertising, on the nightly news (arguably pitched largely as entertainment), or in literature, high and low. The ubiquity of such imagery has the effect of creating a social imagination for which the images are, effectively, true. So, when a young black man is killed by a police officer, we are already primed to assume the former's guilt, or at least that he must have somehow deserved it.

In our nineteenth-century examples above, the social imagination drew from a vast store of imagery related to immigrants, workers, and the poor. Many of the leading figures in the socialist movement of the day were, like August Spies, the speaker at Haymarket, German immigrants. In fact, five of the eight men arrested for the Haymarket Massacre were German immigrants. The comic stereotype of the German male was of a ponderous big-bellied, big-chinned, lager-swilling butcher or bar owner with a thick accent. But this comic image was overshadowed by a much more ominous one, engendering in the American middle class imagination a deep-seated suspicion and fear of "Deinameit Schwartz." A favorite target of the popular press was Johann Most (1846–1906). On release from a German prison for his seditious journalism, Most came to America and threw himself into socialist causes as a newspaper editor and orator. His impassioned speeches in a heavily accented German presented the middle class press with an easy caricature:

---

95 "Cultural Violence," *European Institute for Gender Equality*, https://eige.europa.eu/thesaurus/terms/1070. Accessed July 20, 2020.

His name it was Deinameit Schwartz
He was born in the slums of Berlin.
His beer he demolished in quarts
He possessed large abundance of "chin."
He came to America's shore
With a new patent bomb-shell or ball;
With a thirst for destruction and gore,
And a liver distended with gall.
He was met by ten brazen-tongued bands;
Escorted 'neath banners of red;
And 'mid anarchist shouts and demands
For a speech, to his quarters was led.[96]

The funny, or rather cruelly ridiculous, image of a male Italian immigrant was of an unshaven, droopy mustached, organ grinder or construction worker belting out opera librettos as he works.[97] As with his German comrade, however, the often anarchist leanings of the Italian immigrant rendered him "hot-blooded and volatile, given to quick argument and frequent violence." Even workers and the poor were targeted in the press. Workers were ungrateful men, women, and children, whose ignorant presumption gave them the gall to challenge the domination of the superior middle and upper classes by, for example, demanding an eight-hour workday. The poor were depicted wearing ripped rags as clothing, with ratty disheveled hair, filthy faces, and dirt-stained bare feet. They were characterized as vile, base, lazy, disease-infected, non-humans who earned and deserved every misery and privation that came to them.[98] All of these examples appeared in the burgeoning "humor" magazines of the day. That is to say, they

96 *Texas Siftings,* 6 (June 5, 1886): 9, cited in William R. Linneman, "Immigrant Stereotypes: 1880–1900," *Studies in American Humor*, vol. 1, no. 1 (April 1974): 35-36.
97 Linneman, "Immigrant Stereotypes:" 37.
98 See, Federica Durante and Susan T. Fiske, "How Social-Class Stereotypes Maintain Inequality," *National Institutes of Health*, https://www.ncbi.nlm.nih.gov/pmc/articles/PMC6020691. Accessed July 21, 2020.

appeared, disingenuously, in a form that made their consumption all the readier, namely, in the guise of entertainment:

> Written largely for the urban middle class male, the influence of the illustrated humor periodicals went far beyond their combined 500,000 weekly circulation. They were sold in public places—barbershops, trains, and saloons—and each copy might have several readers. Newspapers clipped their material and spread their opinions further. Their impact on public opinion should not be underestimated. They not only recorded the times, they helped create the times.[99]

So, to review our logic of anarchist violence: *Premise 1. Oppressed people—the poor, wage workers, and politically radical immigrants in our examples—lack faith in "the system."* The reader should be able to infer that anarchism stands on the side of the oppressed. This is true regardless of the social position of the individual anarchist. (If you, too, stand here, you are well-positioned to become a committed anarchist.) *Premise 2. The means of oppression, exploitation, and denial of social goods can be summed up in a word: violence.* This violence, moreover, is not merely the brutal physical, bodily violence of policing, punishment, and prison; it includes insidious everyday forms of structural and cultural violence. So, let's conclude with a question: *Conclusion: "is it not cruel to demand peace from those who are not permitted to live in it?"* And another question: *"A few windows got smashed. Why are 214 people looking at ten years in prison?"* These questions appear in Natasha Lennard's book, *Being Numerous: Essays on Non-Fascist Life.*[100] The first question is Lennard's take on philosopher Bernard Williams's contention that "to say peace when there is no peace is to say nothing." The second question was posed by a twenty-tree-year-old protester at Donald

---

99 Linneman, "Immigrant Stereotypes:" 28.

100 Natasha Lennard, *Being Numerous: Essays on the Non-Fascist Life* (London: Verso, 2019), 87, 88. I am referring to the ebook, whose page numbers may differ from the printed book.

Trump's presidential inauguration, named Olivia Alsip, who, with other protesters, journalists, medics, and legal observers, was brought up on felony riot charges.[101]

Lennard's argument will be instructive to consider, particularly since it brings us up to our own time. While the terms have changed from the nineteenth-century, the logic has remained exactly the same. That is, Mexican, South American, and Arab immigrants have replaced Germans, Italians, Irish as the scourge threatening America. The "poor" has been replaced by "the 99%," those who struggle to keep their heads above financial waters working underpaid and typically meaningless jobs, including often the once secure professional class. The 99% stands in direct contrast to "the 1%," who own nearly as much wealth as everyone else combined.[102] The class consciousness and societal imagination that used to identify "workers" has been obliterated by decades of continuous, often illegal and violent, anti-union activities by employers backed by the state.[103] Thus, "workers," or in Marxist terms,

---

101 The lead prosecutor of the case (or should we say "affair"?), Assistant U.S. Attorney Jennifer Kerkhoff, justified this draconian act as follows: "A person can be convicted of rioting when they themselves have not personally broken a window or personally thrown a rock. It's the group that's the danger. The group that's criminal." Charges against Alsip and most of the other defendants were eventually dropped on the basis of prosecutorial misconduct. Prosecutors failed "to disclose potentially exculpatory evidence to the defense before trial, a violation of the so-called Brady rule." Even more egregiously, they edited out video evidence that was favorable to the defendants. The presiding judge ruled that the Brady violations were "'serious' and 'intentional,' but reserved judgment about whether they were 'malevolent.'" See, Sam Adler-Bell, "With Last Charges Against J20 Protesters Dropped, Defendants Seel Accountability for Prosecutors," *The Intercept*, https://theintercept.com/2018/07/13/j20-charges-dropped-prosecutorial-misconduct. Accessed July 21, 2020.

102 "Comparing the assets of the rich, poor, and middle class," *Economic Research: Federal Reserve Bank of St. Louis*, https://fredblog.stlouisfed.org/2019/10/comparing-the-assets-of-the-rich-poor-and-middle-class. Accessed July 21, 2020.

103 "U.S. employers are charged with violating federal law in 41.5% of all union election campaigns," *Economic Policy Institute*, https://www.epi.org/publication/unlawful-employer-opposition-to-union-election-campaigns. Accessed July 21, 2020. The report of this non-partisan think tank finds: "The data show that U.S. employers are willing to use a wide range of legal and illegal tactics to frustrate the rights of workers to form unions and collectively bargain. Employers are charged with violating federal law

"the proletariat," has been replaced by "the precariat," the growing class of perpetually insecure workers who generate the obscene wealth of corporate America.[104] (Some Covid-19 pandemic-era headlines read: "Jeff Bezos Adds Record $13 Billion in Single Day to Fortune;" and "This is the last week of $600 unemployment benefits."[105]) Interestingly, two terms of fear-mongering derision have remained the same: socialism and anarchism. In the summer of 2020, Donald Trump, in a wall-of-mirrors mashup of nineteenth century anti-radical rhetoric and Richard Nixon's 1968 law and order platform, banked his re-election campaign on inciting fear of anarchists and socialists. His immediate, urgent task was to get "radical-left anarchists" off the streets in the wake of the protests sparked by the police murder of George Floyd. Because anarchists were "doing everything within their power to foment hatred and anarchy," his administration designated antifa a terrorist organization. As Attorney General William Barr put it, "The violence instigated and carried out by antifa and other similar groups in connection with the rioting is domestic terrorism and will be treated accordingly."[106] The longer term intention of the Trump plan is to cast socialism as a dire threat to America. In a recent

in 41.5% of all union election campaigns. And one out of five union election campaigns involves a charge that a worker was illegally fired for union activity. Employers are charged with making threats, engaging in surveillance activities, or harassing workers in nearly a third of all union election campaigns. Beyond this, there are many things employers can do legally to thwart union organizing; employers spend roughly $340 million annually on "union avoidance" consultants to help them stave off union elections. This combination of illegal conduct and legal coercion has ensured that union elections are characterized by employer intimidation and in no way reflect the democratic process guaranteed by the National Labor Relations Act."

104 See Guy Standing, *The Precariat: The New Dangerous Class* (London: Bloomsbury, 2011).

105 *Bloomberg*, https://www.bloomberg.com/news/articles/2020-07-20/jeff-bezos-adds-record-13-billion-in-single-day-to-his-fortune, and CNN, https://www.cnn.com/2020/07/19/politics/unemployment-benefits-economy-congress/index.html, respectively. Accessed July 21, 2020.

106 "Trump Lays Blame for Clashes on 'Radical Left Anarchists,'" *NPR*, https://www.npr.org/2020/05/31/866369727/trump-lays-blame-for-clashes-on-radical-left-anarchists. Accessed July 22, 2020.

speech, his surrogate, Vice President Mike Pence, declared six times with virtually the identical phrase: "My fellow Americans...We have two paths before us: one of freedom and opportunity, the other of socialism and decline."[107] Given the rise and increasing popularity of left-leaning politicians like Alexandria Ocasio-Cortez (D-NY) and Bernie Sanders (I-VT) among young voters, even liberals like House Speaker Nancy Pelosi feel compelled to make clear: "I do reject socialism. If people have that view, that's their view. That is not the view of the Democratic Party." In fact, so far apart are liberals and barely left of liberal Democratic Socialists, that a recent article reported that "Rep. Alexandria Ocasio-Cortez is prepared for the possibility that Democrats in New York could redraw her district after the 2020 election." That's *Democrats*![108]

What is going on here, and what does it have to do with violence? First of all, I want to emphasize that, even if you are reading this manifesto years after it was published, I believe you will discover that, on analysis of your current situation, the *logic* that I am illustrating, if not the actual terms, remains valid. Second of all, I want to warn the reader that what follows may be rough going, and ask only that you read to the end and with an open mind.

According to Lennard, the violence that is endemic to our current situation is an "accident" of liberalism. (It is an intricate argument with a venerable lineage. Here, I can only give a broad sense of what that argument contends.[109]) By "accident," Lennard means something like

---

107 "Remarks by Vice President Pence on the Dangers of Socialism," *The White House*, https://www.whitehouse.gov/briefings-statements/remarks-vice-president-pence-dangers-socialism. Accessed July 21, 2020.

108 Aida Chávez, "New York Democrats Could Eliminate Ocasio-Cortez's District After 2020," *The Intercept*, https://theintercept.com/2019/02/09/ocasio-cortez-district-redistricting-2020. Accessed July 21, 2020.

109 See also, Walter Benjamin, *The Critique of Violence* (link at end); Paul Virilio, *Speed and Violence: An Essay on Dromology* (New York: Semiotext(e), 1977 [1986]) and AK Thompson. *Black Bloc, White Riot* (Oakland: AK Press, 2010). In an interview, AK Thompson says of the latter book: "I argued that black bloc violence was both seductive and disconcerting to the white middle class because it made clear that another sort of

an unintended consequence. For instance, 1.35 million traffic deaths and 50-some million non-lethal injuries per year are an accident of the invention of the automobile; a hole in the ozone layer is an accident of industrialization; the disproportionate murder of young black men by the police is an accident of Enlightenment conceptions of "racial" hierarchies, and so on. As "accidents," such consequences are, she says, "baked into the context." Our current "context" is provided by modern-day liberalism, the kind that is represented by the American Democratic Party. "Liberal centrism," Lennard argues, echoing my own belief, "is conservative." While liberals typically see themselves as socially progressive good guys, the historical record shows that "Many progressive victories claimed by its [i.e., liberalism's] adherents were built on the back, at least in part, of decades-long radical struggles." Such co-opted struggles include women's suffrage, abolition of slavery, an eight-hour workday, abolishing child labor, work safety regulations, civil rights, collective bargaining, and, most recently, Stonewall and LGTBQ rights, and Black Lives Matter. It is typically only in hindsight, long after the risks, and lumps, have been taken and the many loses incurred, that liberals stake a claim in the cause. Lennard is, however, making an even more serious charge against contemporary liberals. She is, namely, implicating their attitudes, beliefs, and ways of being, or "habits," with fascism.

> Unwilling to reckon with the accidents attendant on innovations they otherwise applaud, which are not mistakes, centrist ideologues fail to offer weapons, let alone a sturdy shield, against the fascism of the state, the

---

politics existed beyond representation. Although the black bloc could not move decisively into this new political space, it served as a kind of limit situation for those who remained trapped within the representational sphere. Rather than making demands, black bloc violence tended to open up zones in which new forms of sociality might emerge. In this way, it helped to reveal the intimate connection between violence, production, and politics." Benjamin's text is available online at the *Critical Theory Consortium*: https://criticaltheoryconsortium.org/wp-content/uploads/2018/05/Benjamin-Critique-of-Violence-1.pdf. Accessed July 21, 2020.

> white supremacist constellations it encourages, and the micro-fascisms that permeate daily life and habit.[110]

Her explanation for why liberal ideology does not protect society against fascism is Lennard's most damning contention of all. Its import is bound up in the term "micro-fascisms." "Fascism" here does not denote the large-scale twentieth-century totalitarian regimes of Hitler and Mussolini. It is not used as a political marker of contemporary white supremacist organizations, the neo-Nazi movement, or the alt-right. Neither is it intended to define tendencies within Trump's administration, which, as I write, has sent unidentified federal forces to fight the "ugly anarchists" in Portland, and threatened to do likewise in Chicago, Philadelphia, New York City, Detroit, Baltimore, and Oakland.[111] Fascism *is* all of that, and more—or perhaps, and *less*. Much as I am arguing for anarchism in this manifesto, Lennard contends that these large-scale manifestations of fascism are possible only because of the quotidian "fascistic habit" that conditions so much of our lives in our liberal democracy. Long before this habit results in the desire of the body politic "to dominate, oppress, and obliterate the nameable 'other,'"[112] it manifests as everyday, micro-level domination and oppression, acceptance of hierarchy, respect for law and order, deference to authority, acquiescence to top-down-leadership, and so on. Significantly, the liberal "habit" of fascist tendencies shows up as equivocation concerning the place of violence in the struggle for social change. Given that every single one of the radical victories that I cited

---

110 Lennard, *Being Numerous,* 18.

111 "Portland protests: Trump threatens to send officers to more U.S. cities," *BBC News*, https://www.bbc.com/news/world-us-canada-53481383. Accessed July 21, 2020. His "ugly anarchists" remark was in reference to the autonomous zone created in Seattle in the aftermath of Black Lives Matters protests against the murder of George Floyd by police. *Twitter*, https://twitter.com/realDonaldTrump/status/1271142274416562176?s=20

112 French philosopher Michel Foucault refers to, "The fascism in us all, in our heads and in our everyday behaviour, the fascism that causes us to love power, to desire the very thing that dominates and exploits us." And an anarchist motto goes, "Kill the cop inside your head!" Cited in Lennard, *Being Numerous*, 36 and 38, respectively.

above came in the wake of police batons, tear gas, jailhouse beatings, maiming, concussions, lacerations, incarceration, and death, this equivocation is profoundly revealing.

Lennard provides a litmus test for where a reader might stand on the continuum from liberal-conservative-fascist to socialist-libertarian-anarchist. Do you recall the time that American neo-Nazi leader Richard Spencer was giving an interview to an Australian news crew on the streets of Washington D.C. following the inauguration of Donald Trump? If not, please pause your reading and watch it: https://www.youtube.com/watch?v=aFh08JEKDYk. As you will see, Spencer was sucker-punched hard in his face by a black-clad figure (antifa?) appearing suddenly in the frame. Lennard, who was on the streets demonstrating on that dark, rainy day in January, writes: "I had thought we could all agree: a prominent neo-Nazi was punched in the face; it was a good thing. I had miscalculated 'we.'" So, we can turn Lennard's reaction into a political litmus test: What do you think, *was* it "a good thing"? Lennard reasoned that since the liberal media—*The New York Times*, *The Washington Post*, CNN, MSNBC, NPR, etc.—had been wringing its hands over the fascist tendencies exhibited by the newly installed Trump administration,[113] it would celebrate the unambiguous silencing of a prominent fascist voice. She was dead wrong. The punch "was met with censure from the same liberal media microcosms that had spent the previous weeks nail-biting about fascism."

Why should Lennard be surprised at this outcome of disapproval, and why is it a litmus test of political standing? It has to do with your attitude toward violence. In light of the "Unite the Right" rally in Charlottesville in 2017, where a neo-Nazi drove his car into a crowd of protesters, killing Heather Heyer, "liberal commentators who had [previously] written baseless screeds comparing the threat of far-left anti-fascists to that of white nationalism would surely think twice

113 Lennard lists as such tendencies marked out by the press: "selective populism, nationalism, racism, traditionalism, the deployment of Newspeak and a disregard for reasoned debate," 22.

about such a false equivalency." No, that did not happen. After hearing the president of the United States say, in the aftermath of the confrontation between white nationalists and Charlottesville, that "there's blame on both sides,"[114] Lennard felt certain that the liberal media was about to drop its false equivalency between far-left and far-right violence.

> Instead, it doubled down. In the month that followed the intolerable events in Charlottesville, America's six top broadsheet newspapers ran twenty-eight opinion pieces condemning anti-fascist action, but only twenty-seven condemning neo-Nazis, white supremacists and Trump's failure to disavow them.[115]

What was underway was the predictable process of normalizing fascist tendencies within a liberal democracy, a process that the liberal media had just recently been warning about. This process relied on the "platforming" of, for instance, the "'polite' Midwestern Hitler fan with a Twin Peaks tattoo whose manners 'would please anyone's mother'...the 'dapper' white nationalist,"[116] and, of course, the equally dapper, Ivy-educated, fascist spokesperson son of a doctor and an heiress, Richard Spencer. This is a key element of our litmus test. Should a liberal democracy enable enemies of such basic values as, for instance, equality, inclusion, and multiculturalism, to get so much as a foothold in public discourse? Do you agree with liberal icon Michelle Obama's strategy of going high when they go low? Or do you agree that no amount of liberal appeals to goodness and moral superiority can effectively counter "a fascist epistemology of power and domination—[which] are Spencer and his ilk's first principles."[117] I would like to

---

114 See *PolitiFact* for the entire transcript of Trump's now infamous "good people of both sides" statement, https://www.politifact.com/article/2019/apr/26/context-trumps-very-fine-people-both-sides-remarks. Accessed July 22, 2020.

115 Lennard, *Being Numerous*, 27.

116 Lennard, *Being Numerous*, 28.

117 Lennard, *Being Numerous*, 32.

suggest that we have come to a starkly divided pathway. Equivocation is not neutral. Equivocation is positioned on the side of the status quo. And "the status quo" is the name for a context in which violence is *already* the norm. Anarchist violence, if you accept that premise, is then properly termed "counterviolence," or even more to the point, "impossible nonviolence." It is:

> not an instigation of violence onto a terrain of preexisting peace. A situation in which fascists can gather to preach hate and chant "blood and soil"—this is a background state of violence. The problem we face, then, is not so much that of *necessary violence* as it is one of *impossible nonviolence.*[118]

It is a difficult premise to accept, but bears repeating: the term "fascist" ultimately is not limited to the blatant examples represented by torch-bearing thugs chanting "blood and soil" or by state death cults like Hitler's Nazi Party. Rather, the term is shorthand for insidious "habits" within liberal democracy itself. The most determinate of these habits is also the most difficult for liberals to shake: a commitment to law and order. In this regard, nothing has changed since the days of Auguste Vaillant, Sacco and Vanzetti, and the deed propagandists. As long as the "accidents" of liberalism are with us (capitalism, for instance) the logic of violence will remain valid. Ironically, this is a phenomenon recognized by one of white liberals' favorite go-to figures for issues of social justice. Martin Luther King Jr.'s 1963 "Letter from a Birmingham Jail" is a blistering indictment of the fact that law and order, and the numerous accompanying values and structures that enable it, is baked into American liberal ideology. King wrote his letter in response to another letter, titled "A Call for Unity," written and published openly by eight white clergymen appealing to demonstrators "to observe the principles of law and order and common sense." These clergymen, representing several Christian denominations as well as a rabbi, held the "honest convictions [that] racial matters could properly

118 Lennard, *Being Numerous*, 48.

be pursued in the courts but urged that decisions of those courts should in the meantime be peacefully obeyed." They further held that "hatred and violence have no sanction in our religious and political tradition."[119] King makes two "confessions" concerning his response to the letter. His confessions bear directly on the argument I am making. It will be instructive to quote Dr. King's powerful, eloquent, and absolutely damning first "confession" at length:

> I must confess that over the past few years I have been gravely disappointed with the white moderate. I have almost reached the regrettable conclusion that the Negro's great stumbling block in his stride toward freedom is not the White Citizen's Counciler or the Ku Klux Klanner, but the white moderate, who is more devoted to "order" than to justice; who prefers a negative peace which is the absence of tension to a positive peace which is the presence of justice; who constantly says: "I agree with you in the goal you seek, but I cannot agree with your methods of direct action;" who paternalistically believes he can set the timetable for another man's freedom; who lives by a mythical concept of time and who constantly advises the Negro to wait for a "more convenient season." Shallow understanding from people of good will is more frustrating than absolute misunderstanding from people of ill will. Lukewarm acceptance is much more bewildering than outright rejection.
>
> I had hoped that the white moderate would understand that law and order exist for the purpose of establishing justice and that when they fail in this purpose they become the dangerously structured dams that block the flow of social progress. I had hoped that the white moderate

119 "Alabama Clergymen's Letter *to* Dr. Martin Luther King, Jr." https://tinyurl.com/yyu8orvn. Accessed July 22, 2020. King's response follows.

> would understand that the present tension in the South is a necessary phase of the transition from an obnoxious negative peace, in which the Negro passively accepted his unjust plight, to a substantive and positive peace, in which all men will respect the dignity and worth of human personality. Actually, we who engage in nonviolent direct action are not the creators of tension. We merely bring to the surface the hidden tension that is already alive. We bring it out in the open, where it can be seen and dealt with. Like a boil that can never be cured so long as it is covered up but must be opened with all its ugliness to the natural medicines of air and light, injustice must be exposed, with all the tension its exposure creates, to the light of human conscience and the air of national opinion before it can be cured."[120]

If you are thinking that the logic of violence does not apply to a practitioner of nonviolence, such as King was, I ask you to consider two brief rejoinders. First, as King's metaphor of opening the boil "with all its ugliness" indicates, nonviolence, whether in Gandhi's India, Mandela's South Africa, or King's America, is predicated precisely on the eruption of violence, of violence that already exists, barely below the surface of civility. Violence, in other words, is the necessary condition for effective nonviolence. Second, as Vicky Osterweil notes, the liberal claim that civil rights advances were made because of nonviolence disregards the fact that persistent, seemingly unending, destructive riots played a consequential role in John F. Kennedy's "Report to the American People on Civil Rights,"[121] which led to Lyndon Johnson's

---

120 You can read the original typewritten letter in its entirety online at *The Martin Luther King, Jr. Research and Education Institute*, http://okra.stanford.edu/transcription/document_images/undecided/630416-019.pdf. Accessed July 22, 2020.

121 View Kennedy's speech to the American people: "Report to the American People on Civil Rights," *John F. Kennedy Presidential Library and Museum*, https://www.jfklibrary.org/asset-viewer/report-to-the-american-people-on-civil-rights-11-june-1963. Accessed July 23, 2020.

historic signing of civil rights legislation: "To argue that the movement achieved what it did in spite of rather than as a result of the mixture of not-nonviolent and nonviolent action is spurious at best."[122]

The question is unavoidable: Where do you stand? Recall John Dewey's definition of a liberal as someone with particular "moral attitudes and aspirations." Similarly, this exercise is intended to reveal a stark attitudinal-aspirational *decision*—literally, a cut, or fissure, that lays before us the chasm separating Vaillant and his accusers; Alexander Berkman and Henry Clay Frick, the exploitative chairman of the Carnegie Steel Company Chairman whom Berkman attempted to kill; the Haymarket victims and the state-business nexus that wanted them "wiped out;" George Floyd, Tamir Rice, Michael Brown, Eric Garner, Philando Castile, Breonna Taylor, and 772 other black Americans and the police officers who killed them.[123] This litmus test is intended to force each of us to take a stand on one side or the other; and to do so, if not with consequential action, then at least with our "moral attitudes and aspirations." Can you think of any other way to avoid perpetuating the "great liberal tradition [of standing] on the wrong side of history until that history is comfortably in the past?"[124]

IMPRACTICALITY

What is the good of passing from one untenable position to another, of seeking justification always on the same plane? —Samuel Beckett

As with violence, anarchism names a quite specific species of impracticality. I would even go as far as to claim that anarchism's impracticality is *sui generis,* one of a kind, singular among worldly impracticalities. It is its unique impracticality that makes anarchism salient and vital.

It will be useful to recall two central features of the current text,

---

122 Lennard, *Being Numerous*, 82.

123 See *Statista*. This figure is from 2017 to July 2020. https://www.statista.com/statistics/585152/people-shot-to-death-by-us-police-by-race. Accessed July 22, 2020.

124 Lennard, *Being Numerous*, 29.

mentioned at the outset. The first feature is that this text is written as a manifesto, that is, with the intent to manifest a certain viewpoint within the world, and to persuade as many readers as possible to take seriously that viewpoint. The second feature is that the readers I am mainly hoping to persuade are those who consider themselves politically and socially liberal.

Liberalism is as complex and varied a doctrine as any, and it would be non-productive to enter into a detailed formulation of what I assume "liberalism" means, to you or to anyone else. Broadly, the liberal conception involves three interconnected components: capitalism, government, and the state. A crucial, perhaps *sine qua non*, feature of liberalism is *order*. But wait. Recall that Proudhon prefaced his allegiance to anarchism with "Although a firm friend of order." Clearly, order is an essential, non-negotiable feature of anarchism, too.[125] So, it is crucial to understand the differences between *the nature of order* in the liberal and anarchist worldviews.

My argument is that the liberal conception of order, to which I assume my reader more or less subscribes, consists in and entails features that create *disorder*. Of course, that is exactly the accusation hurled throughout history at anarchism, so a good deal of explanation follows. Let's examine the three interconnected components of liberalism: capitalism, government, and the state.

Liberal justifications of order are, first of all, predicated on the existence of "the market," on, that is, the *laissez-faire* industrial capitalism that was becoming dominant in mid-eighteenth-century England. Theories of (liberal) governance arose at this time largely out of necessity to control a competitive "market" that was proving to be highly volatile, internally contradictory, and fraught with potential widespread societal disaster. The perpetually-threatening disorder of the market was countered with a political "science" that articulated self-serving theories about how (liberal) government could stabilize the ticking time bomb of the market, and sufficiently muffle it when it

125 In the iconic symbol of anarchism, the A encircled by an O, the O signifies "order."

did explode—as it has done dozens and dozens of times since then—as financial crisis, collapse, crash, depression, repression, panic, boom and bust, bubble burst, and outright bankruptcy.[126] And since government itself has proven to be anything *but* the epitome of dependability, the state, finally, is conceived as its, and the market's, ultimate stabilizing remedy. Thus, the "impracticality" of anarchism must be understood against the backdrop of a system that is literally constitutionally incapable of understanding it, much less accommodating it. That is, the ultimate impracticality of anarchism is that it cannot be captured within liberalism's nexus of capitalism-government-state. It thus denies liberalism its most fundamental values, assumptions, and guiding principles. And in offering a lucid, yet radically different, conception of order, anarchism represents a seriously threatening challenge. Whether the reader is willing to see that "the long-standing depiction of anarchism in liberal modes of thought as 'chaotic' [is] a projection of the hidden chaotic core of liberalism itself,"[127] I hope readers will at least consider the merits of anarchism's alternative approach to order, however impractical it appears on the current "plane of justification."

In what follows, I discuss the nexus of capitalism-government-state in terms of the macro-level of politics. But I encourage you to give thought, as you read, to how this nexus operates at the more familiar levels of the meso and the micro. What do you imagine "the state" to denote, for instance, in your workplace? How does "government" function in your friend and family dynamics? How does "capitalism" figure into your life decisions, say, your choice of college or even life partner (or lack thereof)? How does this nexus *order* your actual lived experience and your shared experience with others? Even more importantly, please consider, as you read, just how *practical* these elements of the nexus are. Recall the definition of *practical*: (of an idea, plan, or method) likely to succeed or be effective in real circumstances. Finally,

126 See, for instance, John Kenneth Galbraith, *A Short History of Financial Euphoria* (New York: Penguin Books, 1990).

127 Jimmy Casas Klausen and James Martel, *How Not to be Governed: Readings and Interpretations from a Critical Anarchist Left* (New York: Lexington Books, 2011), xiv.

occasionally ask yourself how your personal and social life would be altered if the nexus were replaced by an anarchist ordering principle.

Capitalism

What is the liberal conception of order? Liberal thinkers debate the proper balance of the three components of capitalism, government, and the state. For example, Austrian economist Ludwig von Mises (1881–1973), perhaps the greatest acolyte of classical (or economic) liberalism since Adam Smith (1723–1790) himself, thought the issue was as clear as the morning bell heralding trade on Wall Street. In his 1927 book *Liberalism: In the Classical Tradition*, von Mises wrote, "The issue is always the same: the government *or* the market. There is no third solution."[128] In other words, "a society in which liberal principles are put into effect is usually called a capitalist society, and the condition of that society, capitalism."[129] This emphasis on "the market/capitalism" is significant because, for this brand of liberalism, the ostensibly socially-beneficent invisible, unencumbered hand of the market, and not any particular form of government *per se*, is, or should be, the determinate factor in our collective social lives. Or, as liberal curmudgeon Thomas Paine put it in 1776, "Society is produced by our wants, and government by our wickedness." Society, whose engine was the emergent capitalism of Paine's day, is an expression of our desires, while government is the necessary check on our, i.e., the market's, "vices."[130]

What is capitalism? The decisive features that distinguish capitalism from other economic systems are: private ownership of the means of production (in capitalist societies, "private" includes both actual individual people and the legally singular "body" or *corpus* known as the "corporation"); statutory protection of private property; financial

128 Ludwig von Mises, *Planned Chaos* (Auburn: *Mises Institute*, 2009 [1951]), 15.

129 "Liberalism and Capitalism," *Mises Institute*, https://mises.org/wire/liberalism-and-capitalism. The first quote is the epigraph on Mises's profile page: https://mises.org/node/42316. Accessed July 28, 2020.

130 Thomas Paine, *Common Sense, Online Library of Liberty*, https://oll.libertyfund.org/pages/1776-paine-common-sense-pamphlet. Accessed August 1, 2020.

incentives to invest profits toward further productive industry; and, following from all of this, the necessity of perpetual growth and expansion. A capitalist economy that is not *growing* is said to be suffering from a slump, recession, depression, malaise, bust, decline, quagmire, crisis. Indeed, even a capitalist economy that is merely "sluggish," much less at a "standstill" or in "stagnation," is considered to be in dire trouble. This emphasis on perpetual growth is instrumental in producing the historically unprecedented wealth of capitalist societies. Growth increases profits and (in theory) the new jobs and higher wages that come with it. From this, it follows that growth also means increased consumer buying capacity and, therefore, overall heightened quality of life. Capitalism is, moreover, more than an economic system. It is the very terrain on which we live our lives. Capitalism has a decisive, indeed determinate, influence on culture, society, and human relationships. (I will return to this point in a moment.) It, arguably more than any other factor in our lives, determines what kind of people we become, or at least, who gets to "succeed" in life. Beginning in elementary school, for example, capitalist societies reward hard work, individualism, competitiveness, productivity, relentlessness, and entrepreneurship. For all of these reasons and more, readers may agree with the 65% of surveyed Americans who view capitalism favorably as the best available system for providing the conditions for individual and social wellbeing.[131] Even if that favorable view could be shown to be misguided, would we not have to agree with one of history's most fervent acolytes of capitalism ever, British Prime Minister Margaret Thatcher, who famously declared "TINA: There Is No Alternative"?[132] There may be no alternative, but, as economist Milton Friedman, another evangelist of market capitalism, wrote, "capitalism is a *necessary* condition for

131 "In Their Own Words: Behind Americans' Views of 'Socialism' and 'Capitalism,'" *PEW Research Center*, https://www.pewresearch.org/politics/2019/10/07/in-their-own-words-behind-americans-views-of-socialism-and-capitalism. Accessed August, 1, 2020.
132 See, Christian Neuhäuser, *TINA*, *Krisis: Contemporary Journal of Philosophy*, https://krisis.eu/wp-content/uploads/2018/07/Krisis-2018-2-Christian-Neuha%CC%88user-TINA.pdf. Accessed August 1, 2020.

political freedom. It is not a *sufficient* condition."[133] In our terms, capitalism is a necessary condition of the liberal conception of order, but it is not sufficient for it.

What else is required? When von Mises presents the dichotomy of "the government *or* the market," he is in part bemoaning the fact that, historically, capitalism and a strong form of government emerged together, joined at the wallet. (Anarchists agree with von Mises on this point, but draw a radically different conclusion from it.) Without the powerful regulation and protection of the government, it was widely argued, human nature would lead to mayhem, chaos, destruction, and perpetual war of all against all. And it would do so in "the market" broadly conceived, that is to say, *everywhere*. An economically-friendly, namely, liberal, form of government would ensure the free functioning of the market together with stabilizing controls. Today, we are witnessing the phenomenon of "illiberal" capitalism in the authoritarian regimes of Russia, Hungary, Poland, Singapore, China, and elsewhere.

Government

This distinction gives us some insight into what today's more *socially* liberal conception of order might broadly entail. To name a few major examples, liberalism and illiberalism are, respectively, for and against: competitive elections, representative governance, judicial independence, separation of powers, rule of law, right of assembly, freedom of the press, protection of civil liberties, and governmental checks and balances. We can extrapolate additional social liberal values from this list. For instance, liberals, in contrast to authoritarian illiberals, more democratically-inclined conservatives, and economic liberals alike, generally believe that the government should play a consequential role in improving our collective quality of life. That is, not only should government wade into the social-cultural mire to help achieve equal opportunity for all, it should function to guarantee that *no one*, ever, is

133 Milton Friedman, *Capitalism and Freedom* (Chicago: University of Chicago Press, 2002 [1962]), 10. Emphases added.

in need of life's essentials. Government, in other words, exists in large part to solve society's problems. We can briefly contrast this view with a conservative conception of order, which places the onus on "the individual." Conservatives generally believe that social, economic, and cultural order is best established and preserved when individuals take ultimate responsibility for their families, neighborhoods, towns and cities, and nation. A limited, minimally engaged government best ensures that people will do so. Government's task is decidedly to steer clear of the social-cultural mire. Its sole purpose is to protect the nation via a strong military, protect the economy via relaxed market regulations, and protect the individual via the championing of traditional values. Paramount among traditional values in the United States, and hence a major concern of American conservatism, is liberty for the individual (hence, "libertarianism" in its rightwing articulation). The government should empower people to partake of their constitution-given freedom to live as they see fit, including solving their own problems. We can extrapolate even more social liberal values from these considerations. For instance, in contrast to conservatives, liberals generally hold the following views: all people, regardless of sexual orientation, should be able to marry under the law; the death penalty should be abolished as cruel and unusual punishment; industrial production is causing rising temperatures and should be reined in regardless of economic costs; the second amendment does not give an *individual* the right to bear arms; healthcare should be universally available and affordable; undocumented immigrants, once here, should be given opportunities, services, and protections; human rights should be protected. Social liberalism differs from economic liberalism, conservatism, and illiberalism in its conception of the relationship between, and not the necessity of, both capitalism and government for the preservation of order.[134] And, like

134 A notorious statement by von Mises gives an indication of economic liberalism's priority: "It cannot be denied that Fascism and similar movements aiming at the establishment of dictatorships are full of the best intentions and that their intervention has, for the moment, saved European civilization. The merit that Fascism has thereby won for itself will live on eternally in history." What fascism "saved" European civilization

them, its conception requires a third component.

Anarchism is "impractical" in the eyes of social liberalism, economic liberalism, conservatism, and illiberalism alike because its logic of order dispenses altogether with the very ground on which their conceptions of order are founded: the state. All existing conceptions of social order, including far left ones like socialism and communism, and far right ones like fascism and totalitarianism, not to mention centrist ones like liberalism and conservatism, share the bedrock conviction that *government must be embedded in the state*.[135] All conceptions of order, that is, but one: anarchism. Anarchism is thus "impractical" only to a system, or person, that is committed to the necessity of *the state*. I am asking my reader to consider the possibility that such a commitment, ideological in nature, profoundly limits our options for social organization. We can consider an instructive parallel (no pun intended): non-Euclidean geometry. The decisive difference between Euclidean and non-Euclidean geometry concerns the behavior of a line. Euclid's fifth postulate assumes parallelism. In upholding this postulate, along with the other four, Euclideans radically limit the field of possible forms. Rejecting this postulate, though preserving the other four, non-Euclidean geometry, by contrast, envisions radical new possibilities; namely, it permits elliptical and hyperbolic curvature. In removing a postulate that was, moreover, not at all self-evident, non-Euclidean geometry is able more accurately to describe actual reality. Might a removal of the state similarly enable us to

---

from was socialism; what it saved it *for* was capitalism. Ludwig von Mises, *Liberalism: In The Classical Tradition*, section I:10, *Mises Institute*, https://mises.org/library/liberalism-classical-tradition/html. Accessed July 29. 2020. In fairness to von Mises, the rest of the quote reads: "But though its policy has brought salvation for the moment, it is not of the kind which could promise continued success. Fascism was an emergency makeshift. To view it as something more would be a fatal error." This does not appear to be the condemnation of fascism that von Mises's allies like to claim. Rather, it suggests, to me, only that the fascism of his day contained elements that, von Mises believed, could not sustain its support of free market capitalism, and hence was ultimately unsuitable.

135 Yes, a dogma of Marxism is that the state will eventually "wither away." Yet, it never does.

envision radically new and eminently *practical*, because *more realistic*, possibilities for social organization?

The State

What is "the state"? The first thing to say is that the state is *not* the government. This fact is of crucial significance because anarchism, contrary to its popular caricature, is *not* anti-government—if, that is, we conceive of "government" as involving social organization subtracted from the statist postulate of order. In brief, the state is:

> A form of human association distinguished from other social groups by its purpose, the establishment of order and security; its methods, the laws and their enforcement; its territory, the area of jurisdiction or geographic boundaries; and finally, by its sovereignty.[136]

Like the Golem we met earlier, the state is a human-made abstraction, a fiction with real life effects. In my survey of the literature, it does not appear, for example, to be a controversial view that "The modern territorial state is a product of jurists; it was created by jurists in the sixteenth century; it has been later developed by jurists."[137] What I hope to challenge here is the unquestioned assumption among social liberals that it is indeed a *necessary* fiction.

The modern concept of the state as a necessary fiction emerged only in the sixteenth century. The impetus for its articulation is captured in the motivation behind jurist Jean Bodin's (1530-1596) groundbreaking theory of sovereignty:

> The bitter experience of civil war and its attendant anarchy in France had turned Bodin's attention to the problem of how to secure order and authority. Bodin thought that the

136 *Encyclopedia Britannica*, *s.v.*, State, https://www.britannica.com/topic/state-sovereign-political-entity. Accessed July 30, 2020.

137 Sabino Cassese. "The Rise and Decline of the Notion of State," *International Political Science Review / Revue Internationale De Science Politique* 7, no. 2 (1986): 121.

> secret lay in recognition of the sovereignty of the state and argued that the distinctive mark of the state is supreme power. This power is unique; absolute, in that no limits of time or competence can be placed upon it; and self-subsisting, in that it does not depend for its validity on the consent of the subject.[138]

Hence, Bodin's statist postulate: "Majesty or sovereignty is the most high, absolute, and perpetual power over the citizens and subjects in a Commonwealth, which the Latins call *Majestas*." The location of this sovereignty is precisely "the state." Indeed, Bodin's immediate goal was to establish ultimate sovereignty in His Majesty King Henry III (1551–1589) during the Huguenot rebellion.[139] Not long thereafter, King Louis XIV (1638–1715) famously proclaimed with utter confidence, "L'etat c'est moi" ("*I* am the state"). Niccolo Machiavelli (1469–1557), another founding figure of the modern conception of the state, also contended that "the only real concern of the political ruler is the acquisition and maintenance of power." Contrary to the prevailing notion of his day that the ruler must be the very embodiment of such virtues as justice, honesty, equanimity, and good-heartedness, Machiavelli held that, to be effective, a ruler must be constitutionally (in both senses of the term) capable of forgoing virtue in order to fulfill his or her primary function: unshakable stability of the state. What justified such a dominating, controlling, and unassailable entity? In a justification that we will return to later, Machiavelli famously contends:

> One can say this in general of [people]: they are ungrateful, disloyal, insincere and deceitful, timid of danger and avid of profit...Love is a bond of obligation which these miserable creatures break whenever it suits them to do so; but

138 Mario Turchetti, "Jean Bodin", *The Stanford Encyclopedia of Philosophy*, https://plato.stanford.edu/archives/fall2018/entries/bodin. Accessed July 30, 2020.

139 An excellent analysis of Bodin's concept is William A. Dunning. "Jean Bodin on Sovereignty." *Political Science Quarterly* 11, no. 1 (1896): 82-104.

> fear holds them fast by a dread of punishment that never passes.[140]

As the mechanism of holding fast the brutish populace, the statist postulate was bolstered by such influential notions as Thomas Hobbes's (1588–1679) that "there is no society as distinct from the state," and Georg Hegel's (1770–1831) that the state "is an organism in which the life of the parts is embodied," including, we should recall, the parts called "government" and "the market."[141]

The Liberal Worldview

So, to review, the liberal conception of order assumes the necessity to the economic system of (i) capitalism because of its productive power, (ii) a form of government that best facilitates the functioning of the economy, and (iii) a concept of the sovereign state to stabilize the government and hold it accountable to its stewardship of the economy. The state, again, is a particular "form of human association" whose purpose is to establish order and security within a defined geographical territory. The "jurisdiction" that it claims within this territory is established in laws, and enforced by courts and policing. The state distinguishes itself from all other political entities through its assertion of ultimate sovereignty. The state, again, is not the government. The government is a temporary body that derives its power *from* the state. In the United States, for instance, a presidential inauguration is the ritualized conferring of state power to the chief of the executive branch of government, if only for a "term." Similar rituals are performed for members of the legislative and judicial branches. Power thus conferred, the government may legitimately function as the machine of the state. When members of an administration complain of hidden machinations of the "deep state," they are acknowledging,

---

140 Cary Nederman, "Niccolò Machiavelli,"*The Stanford Encyclopedia of Philosophy*, https://plato.stanford.edu/archives/sum2019/entries/machiavelli. Accessed July 30, 2020.

141 Sabino Cassese. "The Rise and Decline of the Notion of State, 121.

and bemoaning, a temporal and hierarchical priority. Similarly, when the Attorney General undermines the decisions of "career prosecutors," as happened repeatedly under William Barr, what is at stake is not merely the livelihood of a few individuals; it is nothing less than "the rule of law," that is to say, state sovereignty, itself.[142] Government officials take an oath to "support and defend the Constitution of the United States," to uphold, that is, the sovereignty of the state over any particular government in which they may be serving. Finally, as we see every four years in a presidential election season, if the state's main purpose is to stabilize the government, one of the primary concerns of the government is to stabilize the vibrant humming of "the economy, stupid."[143]

I would wager that, at minimum, my reader agrees with Thomas Paine that "Clearly Government, even in its best state, is a necessary evil."[144] I would take it even further and bet that readers just may believe that, like the devil we know, liberal, representative "democracy is the worst form of government except for all the others that have been tried," as Winston Churchill famously opined.[145] I would wager further that my reader is not inclined to conceive of a viable

---

142 See, for instance, Elliott B. Jacobson, "It's Clear: Attorney General William Barr Must Go," *New York Law Journal*, https://www.law.com/newyorklawjournal/2020/06/25/it-is-clear-attorney-general-william-barr-must-go. Accessed July 31, 2020.

143 See, Julian Zelizer, "'It's the economy, stupid' all over again," *CNN*, https://www.cnn.com/2020/05/08/opinions/economy-2020-election-trump-biden-zelizer/index.html. Accessed August 1, 2020. Bill Clinton's political strategist during the 1984 election, James Carville, "famously reminded his team in the campaign war room, 'It's the economy, stupid!' whenever anyone veered off track." The "track" was the fact that George Bush was trailing in the polls largely because of the economic recession. The actual role that the state of the economy plays in elections is debated by scholars. See, Danielle Kurtzleben, "The Economy May Be Losing Its Impact On Presidential Elections," *NPR*, https://www.npr.org/2020/07/09/889080504/the-economy-may-be-losing-its-impact-on-presidential-elections. Accessed August 1, 2020.

144 Thomas Paine, *Common Sense, Online Library of Liberty*, https://oll.libertyfund.org/pages/1776-paine-common-sense-pamphlet. Accessed August 1, 2020.

145 In Larry Jay Diamond and Marc F. Plattner, *Democracy: A Reader* (Baltimore: Johns Hopkins University Press, 2009), 244.

alternative to capitalism. Finally, because I write this in the heat of Donald Trump's flagrant lawlessness and corruption, I would wager that my reader is hopeful that the sovereignty of the state will ultimately prevail.[146]

146 Read this remarkable "Memorandum of Law" which refers to "public reports of possibly extensive and protracted criminal conduct" (p.17) by the Trump Organization, http://cdn.cnn.com/cnn/2020/images/08/03/da.response.to.vance.pdf. Accessed August 4, 2020.

4.
An Anarchist's Perspective

My own hope, of course, is that something other than the state ultimately prevails such that a Donald Trump never again comes anywhere near the seat of government. Or, more to the point, my hope—an anarchist's hope—is that Donald Trumps cease to exist at all. That is, contrary to Machiavelli's assertion above that the state is absolutely essential because people are inherently "ungrateful, disloyal, insincere and deceitful, timid of danger and avid of profit," anarchists are wary of such essentialist notions of human nature, and so tend to believe that society generally, and education specifically, are the decisive determinants of human dispositions. Arguably, "Donald Trump," like "Citizen Kane" and "The Great Gatsby," names nothing if not an exemplar of the crass excess that is the capitalist subject. Being an anti-idealist, indeed a radically materialist ideology, anarchism holds that the capitalist subject is *forged*, created, formed, precisely in the crucible of the social nexus, where capitalism, government, and the state converge. In my usage of Beckett's question in the previous section's epigraph, this crucible is the very "plane" on which we continually forge "one untenable position" after another. Worse, once the new untenable position is forged, its very "justification" is then sought and secured on precisely "the same plane."

Why do anarchists hold that this situation, *our* situation within the current social nexus, is untenable? Why do they further believe that justifying any new position yet again on that plane is a losing proposition? Let's look at how capitalism, government, and the state appear from an anarchist perspective. Let me quickly remind the reader that the purpose of a manifesto is not to construct a thorough critique of some subject, but rather to make clear a quite specific idea, and to persuade readers to adopt that idea. Or, in the spirit of Beckett, the purpose is to incite you to make a change of plane.

AN ANARCHIST'S CRITIQUE OF CAPITALISM

Let's begin with capitalism. In a talk titled "Why Capitalism Is Toxic to the Environment," environmentalist Fred Bagdoff, bluntly states a general truth:

> It is important to keep in mind that the purpose of the capitalist economic system is not to provide the basic needs for all people, not to provide jobs for everyone that wants to work, not to protect the environment. As ecologist Richard Levins has put it: "Agriculture is not about producing food but about profit. Food is a side effect...Health service is a commodity, health a byproduct."[147]

Let's ignore the dubiousness that what industrialized agriculture produces is best categorized as "food,"[148] or that the obvious byproduct of the American health care industry is "health."[149] The purpose of capitalism is, obviously, to make money in order to make more money

---

147 Fred Bagdoff, "Why Capitalism Is Toxic to the Environment," *Radical Education Pamphlet*, http://physics.bu.edu/~pankajm/Activism/FinishedPamphlets/magdoff-pamphlet.pdf. Accessed August 1, 2020.

148 See, for instance, "The Industrialisation of Food Creates Unease," *alimentarium*, https://www.alimentarium.org/en/magazine/society/industrialisation-food-creates-unease. Accessed August 7, 2020. Main takeaway: "Our relationship with food is intrinsically troubled, both owing to the need to secure supplies as well as due to the risk of intoxication."

149 See, for instance, "American Healthcare is Sick, and its Workers are, Too." *Scientific American*, https://blogs.scientificamerican.com/observations/american-health-care-is-sick-and-its-workers-are-too. Accessed August 7, 2020. Main takeaway: "The health care delivery system both reflects society's ills and reinforces them."

in order to make even more money in order to...literally *ad infinitum*. It does this in the first instance by incentivizing businesses to create commodities, or purchasable objects, out of every conceivable thing under the sun, even abstractions like learning ($122,000 on average per U.S. student for a four-year degree[150]) and love ($72 billion a year wedding industry;[151] $18 billion for engagement rings[152]). Even more insidiously, capitalism creates *desire* for its objects. Let's look at a commodity that many people today reflexively believe to be an essential feature of the marriage process, indeed of "true love" itself: the engagement ring.

Prior to September 1938, virtually no man possessed a desire to express his (it became a gendered matter, too) love by slipping a shiny diamond ring on his beloved's finger. And even if he had, virtually no woman had a desire to have it slipped on. Until, that is, Harry met Gerold. Harry Oppenheimer was the son of the founder of the world's preeminent diamond mining company, De Beers, in South Africa. Gerold M. Lauck was the president of a preeminent American advertising agency, N. W. Ayer, founded in Philadelphia. In short, what this meeting produced was the "diamond invention—the creation of the idea that diamonds are rare and valuable, and are essential signs of esteem."[153] To be profitable, the "invention" further required the creation of a new human desire: to possess a diamond ring. So, over the next fifty years, De Beers would increase its advertising budget from a paltry $200,000 to $10,000,000 a year. The result was a boom in diamond ring sales from $23 million to $2.1 billion. How did the Ayer agency achieve this remarkable result? Well, first things first. What is an advertising campaign without a catchy slogan? Faced with the

150 *Education Data*, https://educationdata.org/average-cost-of-college. Accessed August 3, 2020.

151 *Fast Company*, https://tinyurl.com/y36s9qpf. Accessed August 3, 2020.

152 *Vogue Magazine*, https://tinyurl.com/y3lkolbc. Accessed August 3, 2020.

153 In this section on the diamond "invention," I am referring to and citing Edward Jay Epstein, "Have You Ever Tried to Sell a Diamond?," *The Atlantic*, https://www.theatlantic.com/magazine/archive/1982/02/have-you-ever-tried-to-sell-a-diamond/304575. Accessed August 3, 2020.

harsh fact that in the United States, the battlefield of the De Beers/Ayer campaign, "the quality of diamonds, measured in dollar value, had declined by nearly 100 percent" in recent years, the agency came up with a slogan for the ages: "A Diamond is Forever."[154] Brilliant! The insinuation, of course, is that both the love and the object that symbolizes that love are indestructible. And just in case that love, despite the magical incantation of the slogan, somehow falters and fades, the timeless rarity and value of the diamond would forever insure that it was, at least, an excellent *financial* investment. What I am about to say will matter not one whit to the love birds of the world. It is, however, significant to our purpose here. And that is: *the desire for a diamond ring is founded on a lie*. Diamonds are neither rare, valuable, nor lasting. *Not lasting*: Believe it or not, our symbol of eternal love is "very brittle."[155] It can be "shattered, chipped, discolored, or incinerated to ash."[156] In scientific terms, diamonds are merely "metastable," that is "not stable, *stricto sensu*."[157] (A symbol of the actual state of "true love" after all?) *Not valuable*: As the title of the article to which I am referring here implies—"Have You Ever Tried To Sell A Diamond?"—outside of the industry itself, diamonds possess virtually no value.

> When thieves bring diamonds to underworld "fences," they usually get only a pittance for them. In 1979, for example, New York City police recovered stolen diamonds with an insured value of $50,000 which had been sold to a "fence" for only $200.[158]

---

154 The slogan, written by, Ayers copywriter Mary Frances Gerety, was named the slogan of the century in 1999. by *Advertising Age*. https://adage.com/article/special-report-the-advertising-century/ad-age-advertising-century-top-10-slogans/140156. Accessed August 4, 2020.

155 Sami Mikhail, "The Science Behind your Diamond Ring (And Why It's Not Forever!)," *Refinery29*, https://www.refinery29.com/en-gb/diamonds-are-forever-science. Accessed August 3, 2020.

156 Epstein, "Have You Ever Tried to Sell a Diamond?"

157 Sami Mikhail, "The Science Behind your Diamond Ring."

158 Epstein, "Have You Ever Tried to Sell a Diamond?"

Like those Las Vegas bookies who set odds on this or that event's happening, sadly, and quite bizarrely, thieves operating on the black market apparently have a more honest approach to diamond appraisal than does your local De Beers expert. It certainly makes you wonder who the real thieves are here. Or, to paraphrase Bertold Brecht's biting query about the inherent criminality of banks: What is the crime of *robbing* a diamond store to the crime of *founding* one? But, can we really call it a crime when the victim of the theft initiates and encourages, indeed, *desires*, the robbery? We will return to this question in a moment. To continue. *Not rare*: Here is an extraordinary matter-of-fact statement by none other than Diamond Foundry, the company that is "delivering the future of diamonds" around the world: "Contrary to common belief, diamonds are not rare inside Earth. There are vast resources of diamonds inside the Earth—scientists now estimate that a quadrillion tons of diamonds lie deep beneath the Earth's surface."[159] That's a thousand million millions of *tons*—not individual pieces, *tons*—of diamonds. Ants, trees, and potatoes, like virtually every other object under the sun, are rarer than diamonds.

How can such a ruse occur? How can consumers be led to desire an object whose very desirability is rooted in such glaring illusion? With this question, I want to encourage my reader to consider the contention that deeper layers of capitalist insidiousness are operating, such that the deception, indeed the theft, that occurs with the simple purchase of an engagement ring occurs at "the market" in broad daylight, so to speak, on the very "plane" of the social nexus that we are investigating. The explanation is quite simple. Capitalism is a desiring-production machine. It creates simultaneously the desire and the object to satisfy that desire. It does so through a mechanism that is so dependably effective in its aim that capitalists, government officials, and state agents embrace it with equal fervor. This mechanism is called by turns propaganda, mind control, emotional manipulation, hidden persuasion,

159 https://diamondfoundry.com/blogs/the-foundry-journal/are-diamonds-rare-1. Accessed August 3, 2020.

manipulation of motives, impulse control, crowd manipulation, and spin. The inventor of the mechanism called it "psychological warfare." Today, we know it as "public relations," or simply, "advertisement." The figure behind this mechanism was none other than Sigmund Freud's American nephew, Edward Bernays (1891–1995). This kinship is not a mere coincidence. Like his psychoanalysis-founding uncle, Bernays was convinced that people are unsuspecting manipulable creatures, driven, as they are, principally by needs, wants, fears, hopes, wishful thinking, and desires that answer sooner to the irrational demands of the unconscious than to lucid conscious reasoning. Bernays's writings include such telling tomes as *The Engineering of Consent*, *Crystallizing Public Opinion*, and, of course, *Propaganda*. (After World War II, Bernays received unrelenting pushback on his preferred term "propaganda," and so begrudgingly changed it to "public relations," itself a brilliant act of propaganda.) In the latter book, on page after page, the founder of public relations unabashedly says the secret part out loud. For example:

> The conscious and intelligent manipulation of the organized habits and opinions of the masses is an important element in democratic society. Those who manipulate this unseen mechanism of society constitute an invisible government which is the true ruling power of our country. We are governed, our minds are molded, our tastes formed, and our ideas suggested, largely by men we have never heard of...It is they who pull the wires that control the public mind.[160]

Bernays was no mad scientist, toiling in obscurity. Neither was he serving up a conspiracy theory. Politicians quickly came to recognize that his method for pulling wires could be true for the actual, visible government as well. Presidents Calvin Coolidge and Dwight Eisenhower employed Bernays in what, in our time, would become the

160 Edward Bernays, *Propaganda* (Brooklyn: IG Publishing, 1928), 37.

common practice of political blandishment. Apparently the man whose ideas attracted the attention of Nazi Germany propaganda minister Josef Goebbels did at least have his scruples.[161] Bernays reports that he had turned down offers to work his magic from such luminaries as the German Nazi Party, the rightwing government of Nicaragua, the rightwing Spanish dictator Francisco Franco, and a Vice President Richard Nixon on the verge of his first presidential run.[162] That these hopeful clients called on the public relations wizard at all, however, is instructive in itself. It points to the fact that Bernays had indeed developed an effective technique to "engineer" the docile and unknowing consent of the masses. To get a basic sense of how one might go about doing so, we can take a quick look at how the Ayers agency strategically went about "strengthen[ing] the tradition of the diamond engagement ring—to make it a psychological necessity" as its report to De Beers put it.[163] First, as good disciples of Bernays (and Freud), they acknowledged that "We are dealing with a problem in mass psychology."[164] Then, they commenced to engineer consent. How? Simple. They conjured in their female "target audience" (lots of martial metaphors in marital advertising) of "some 70 million people 15 years and over" the as yet non-existent desire for "diamond rings as symbols of romantic involvement." They arranged for speakers to address "thousands of girls in their assemblies, classes, and informal meetings in our leading educational institutions." (That sounds incredible until you consider that military recruiters employ the exact same strategy today.[165]) In

---

161 In his autobiography, *Biography of an Idea: The Founding Principles of Public Relations*, Bernays was told from someone with firsthand knowledge that Bernays's *Crystalizing Public Opinion* was in Goebbels's "propaganda library." When he heard this, Bernays says he was "shocked," and added, "but I knew that any any human activity can be used for social purposes and misused for antisocial ones." *Google Books*, np.

162 Larry Tye, *The Father of Spin: Edward L. Bernays and the Birth of Public Relations* (New York: Crown, 1998,) 88–89.

163 Epstein, "Have You Ever Tried to Sell a Diamond?"

164 Epstein, "Have You Ever Tried to Sell a Diamond?"

165 See, "The Military Targets Youth for Recruitment, Especially at Poor Schools," *Teen Vogue*, https://www.teenvogue.com/story/the-military-targets-youth-for-recruitment.

newspapers and magazines, they placed articles, notices, and images of celebrities wearing diamonds—movie stars, socialites, entertainers, the wives and daughters of politicians—of, that is, "any woman who can make the grocer's wife and the mechanic's sweetheart say *I wish I had what she has.*"[166]

I am using this example of the diamond engagement ring and the mechanism by which it is rendered desirable to illustrate a larger, indeed virtually universal, feature of our lives under capitalism. A succinct, if somewhat opaque, expression of this universal feature is found in Proposition #16 of Guy Debord's 1967 *Society of the Spectacle*:

> The spectacle subjugates living [people] to itself to the extent that the economy has totally subjugated them. It is no more than the economy developing for itself. It is the true reflection of the production of things, and the false objectification of the producers.[167]

The reader may understandably resist being reduced to a puppet whose wires are being pulled by "the spectacle," and, moreover, being pulled for the sole purpose of developing *not* societal wellbeing, not personal happiness or health, but merely *the market itself.* If this sounds like an outrageous conspiracy theory, I hope the reader will consider the following assertions. "Spectacle" is an apt metaphor for life in a capitalist society. It suggests that we are mesmerized, infatuated, spellbound, bewitched, beguiled, and eventually seduced by a perpetually unfolding market extravaganza of commodities, images, and representations, the overwhelming majority of which are demonstrably superfluous, indeed often counterproductive, to happiness and wellbeing. Debord was writing in the days when "mass media" meant the slow, intermittent consumption of film, television, radio, magazines, and newspapers. Given the omnipresence of the internet, how much more

---

Accessed August 5, 2020.

166 Epstein, "Have You Ever Tried to Sell a Diamond?" Emphasis added.

167 Guy Debord, *Society of the Spectacle*, https://www.marxists.org/reference/archive/debord/society.htm. Accessed August 4, 2020.

inundating is this hyper-accelerated desire-producing consumer-corporationist market in our lives today?

One last point for reflection. We are exploring the common perception that anarchism, as a set of ideas concerning social organization, is impractical. Returning to our example of the diamond engagement ring, we can consider the "practicality" of this single item. However, I would ask the reader to extend this consideration to include *virtually everything produced under capitalism.* That is, if the production of even an innocuous object like a ring can be shown to be impractical, where do we draw the line? What if, with a minimum of honest, informed reflection, we begin to see virtually all objects in the light of their ultimate impracticality? And what if this impracticality were a result not of the objects themselves but of the very mode of their production, distribution, and ultimate disposal? That is to say, what if we came to the conclusion that the ultimate "impracticality" has to do with capitalism itself? Worse, if we accept my contention, even in a passing thought-experiment, that capitalism is an integral and overdetermining element in the economy-government-state nexus, how might this impracticality bode for our very lives, today and into the future? Finally, what if the term "impracticality," which is routinely thrown out, along with "violence," as a feature that now and forever disqualifies anarchism from intelligent consideration of viable ideas, turns out to be an understatement with historically disastrous consequences?

In the talk I mentioned earlier, "Why Capitalism Is Toxic to the Environment," Fred Bagdoff quotes Naomi Klein making a deeply disconcerting point: "leftists...have yet to recognize that the ecological crisis is the highest expression of the capitalist threat" and that even "environmentalists...imagine we can solve the ecological crisis without confronting capitalism." What makes this statement so troubling is that the very people who should be the most clear-eyed about the overarching impact of the capitalist system of production somehow fail to see it. Ever since Marx's epoch-making analysis in *Capital* (1867), capitalism has been front and center as *the* culprit in social and ecological devastation.[168] How could "leftists" fail to see this relationship? You also have to wonder how capitalism's role in the ecological disaster has been missed by the *environmentalist* analysis. Perhaps Mark Fisher's characterization of capitalism as a 'pervasive atmosphere…acting as a kind of invisible barrier constraining thought and action," serves as a partial explanation. In any case, let's further consider the case of the diamond engagement ring.

Originating in a high-pressure furnace one hundred miles below the earth's upper mantel, many diamond crystals, due to ancient deep-seated volcanic eruptions, have been displaced to higher, accessible, regions of the earth's surface.[169] Still, in order to find a tiny piece of rough diamond, 1,750 tons—*tons*—of earth have to be extracted.[170] This excavation, of course, is often preceded by massive logging, deforestation, and displacement of animals and peoples. But let's put that aside. The removal of earth alone creates a crater equaling the depth of ten Empire State Buildings, rendering infeasible the mine's legal obligation to return the stripped earth as close as possible to its original state. Let's jump to the ring part of the equation. For, to be alchemically transmuted into the desire-eliciting object with the spectral representation of lasting romantic love, the rough one-carat diamond crystal must be transformed into the cultural artifact known as a "ring." The minute amount of gold or silver required to produce the small band into which the diamond is typically placed generates twenty tons

168 See, for instance, "Karl Marx: Radical Environmentalist," *Socialist Worker*, https://tinyurl.com/y4nnq4vy. Accessed August 8, 2020. Marx writes, for example: "Capitalist production, by collecting the population in great centers, and causing an ever-increasing preponderance of town population, on the one hand concentrates the historical motive power of society; on the other hand, it disturbs the circulation of matter between man and the soil, i.e., prevents the return to the soil of its elements consumed by man in the form of food and clothing; it therefore violates the conditions necessary to lasting fertility of the soil."

169 "Diamonds Unearthed," *Smithsonian Magazine*, https://tinyurl.com/y4wv3wuc. Accessed August 8, 2020.

170 Unless otherwise noted, in this part I am referring to the website *The Greener Diamond* for this information, http://thegreenerdiamond.org/conflict-diamonds-2/environmental-impact. Accessed August 8, 2020.

of toxic waste material. That's not all: "The earth-mined ore is mixed with cyanide, a known toxic poison, to dissolve the gold or silver from the ore, making the land and waterways around the mining area poisoned." Fortunately, Canada, the world's fifth largest diamond-mining country, has introduced "conflict-free" mines with the explicit intent of minimizing this environmental damage. Maybe capitalism can correct its worst excesses after all!

> Canadian diamonds are more popular with buyers because they are not classed "blood diamonds" like their African counterparts, where environmental protection regulations and worker interests are often severely compromised.[171]

Great! So, some quick facts about this benevolent enterprise. First, these "conflict-free" mines "are often built in environmentally fragile ecosystems," leave "significant ecological footprints," and, it follows, "significantly impact upon the caribou, wolverine, bears, ptarmigan and fish which provide food for Aboriginal peoples." The equivalent of "40 Olympic-sized swimming pools per day or 14,600 per year" are pumped out of the mine pit and into the local river. Over time, the flow of that river "will be decreased by at least 15%, harming fish populations." The nearly 30 tons of rock that must be dug up and dumped outside the mining area will likely "leak chemicals, such as acids, into the surrounding waters." The obvious question arises: who or what is avoiding conflict in this conflict-free approach?

Is it not clear that not only is the production of diamond engagement rings impractical, it is outright *unsustainable*. "Unsustainability" is the word of the moment when it comes to analyzing the cost of capitalist production. Not only is the capitalist system inherently unstable, it is inherently unsustainable. It is, moreover, unsustainable in both senses of the term. It literally cannot continue to function at its current rate because of resource depletion; and it is indefensible,

---

171 *NS Energy* website, https://www.nsenergybusiness.com/news/top-diamond-mining-countries-world. Accessed August 8, 2020.

like a flawed argument whose flaws and contradictions collapse it from within. I encourage the reader to do even the briefest research on the costs—human, animal, and environmental; physical, psychological, and emotional—of producing such "necessities" as, say, the cell phone,[172] or such symbols of wholeness as a glass of milk.[173] Why not add to your list such everyday items as computers and the internet, cars and driving, meat and poultry, air travel, electricity, scrambled eggs, a college education, and anything else that pops into your to mind? You won't have to navigate your online search toward lefty sites like *People's Daily*, either. Stalwart champions of capitalism like *The Economist*, *The New York Times*, and even *Forbes* admit the problem. In a recent *Forbes* article titled, "Unless It Changes, Capitalism Will Starve Humanity By 2050," we are told in no uncertain terms that: Capitalism has "devastated the planet and has failed to improve human well-being at scale;" the extinction rate of entire species is "1,000 times faster than that of the natural rate over the previous 65 million years;" 14,826,322 acres of primary forest (i.e., forest area containing tree species native to the land, and where natural ecological processes have not yet been

172 For instance, workers "as young as 10 years old dig for tin, tantalum, and tungsten," the main minerals needed to produce the smartphone, "making an average of $1 a day in an environment lacking in health or safety standards." Most of the waste from discarded smartphones "ends up in a landfill where harmful chemicals can leak into groundwater and affect both human and plant life. By 2020, it's estimated that the EU will generate more than 12 million tonnes per year...Still heavily dependent on fossil fuels, the manufacturing process generates waste that is 200 times the weight of the phone." See, "The Social and Environmental Impact of Mobile Phones," *Reset: Digital for Good*, https://tinyurl.com/y6m5lvp2. Accessed August 8, 2020.

173 For instance, in a world of diminishing water supplies, it takes 2,000 gallons of water to produce one gallon of milk. So, in drinking that milk, you are effectively dumping out 1,999 gallons of water. But it's healthy, right? "When you drink milk, you are literally consuming blood and pus from an animal that has been abusively milked and pumped up with artificial hormones. These hormones are banned in almost every other country in the world but remain legal in the United States." That's not even to mention the "run-off poisoning of our rivers, streams and oceans from pesticides, herbicides and synthetic drugs pumped into cows" that produce our milk. See, *Natural News* website, https://www.naturalnews.com/023341_water_milk_organic.html. Accessed August 8, 2020.

noticeably impacted by humans) have been lost each year since 2000 (that's roughly the size of West Virginia each year); in the U.S. alone, 15% of the population lives below the poverty line, and for children under the age of 18, that number increases to 20% (that's around 73 million children, roughly the equivalent of the entire populations of the United Kingdom and Bulgaria combined).[174] This is *Forbes*, not *Socialist Worker*, that concludes: "Corporate capitalism is committed to the relentless pursuit of growth, even if it ravages the planet and threatens human health."

I feel confident saying that none of the captains of capitalism we have encountered here would take issue with Magdoff's, Klein's, *Forbes's*, or my own assertions. The market-fawning website *Investopedia* provides a validation for my confidence when even it, in its cautiously value-neutral overview of capitalism, has to admit that "the real-world practice of capitalism typically involves some degree of so-called 'crony capitalism.'"[175] The "cronies" here are, of course, the three entities that we are examining in this section, namely, the business class, the political class, and the state class. Capitalism does not thrive because of the blinding brilliance of the geniuses who run our corporations and industries. It "thrives" because of the steady stream of political favors granted those people: lax regulations, tax breaks, special grants, low interest loans, debt forgiveness, bailouts, special exemptions, refusal to enact laws around living wages and essential benefits for employees, and so on.[176] Indeed, crony capitalism, if not necessarily an integral fea-

---

174 Drew Hanson, "Unless It Changes, Capitalism Will Starve Humanity By 2050," *Forbes*, https://www.forbes.com/sites/drewhansen/2016/02/09/unless-it-changes-capitalism-will-starve-humanity-by-2050/#182ee7877ccc. Accessed August 8, 2020.

175 *Investopedia*, https://www.investopedia.com/terms/c/capitalism.asp. Accessed August 1, 2020.

176 Martin Luther King, Jr. famously noted in 1968 that in America it's "socialism for the rich and rugged free enterprise capitalism for the poor." His observation is borne out in *Pro Publica's* "Bailout Tracker," an incredible list of 975 companies that have recently received three quarters of a trillion dollars of what can only be termed "corporate welfare" from the United States government. We are not talking mom and pop stores. The list leads off with none other than the Bank of America, J.P. Morgan, Citigroup, AIG, Wells

ture, is "the dominant form of capitalism worldwide." This is according to *Investopia*, a pro-capitalist platform whose motto is "Sharper Insight. Better Investing." Given the fact that in capitalist societies, as we saw, the government exists largely to keep "the market" humming, what should we expect?

AN ANARCHIST'S CRITIQUE OF GOVERNMENT-STATE

With the invocation of "crony capitalism," we have come full circle, back to our original "plane of justification." For, similar to my claim about capitalism's unsustainability, I am confident that none of our corporate and industry CEOs would dispute the symbiotic relationship formed in the capitalist-government-state nexus.[177] Before examining the

---

Fargo, Goldman Sachs, and so on. https://projects.propublica.org/bailout/list. Accessed August 1, 2020. King's quote is worth giving in full: "Whenever the government provides opportunities and privileges for white people and rich people they call it 'subsidized' when they do it for Negro and poor people they call it 'welfare.' The fact is, everybody in this country lives on welfare. Suburbia was built with federally subsidized credit. And highways that take our white brothers out to the suburbs were built with federally subsidized money to the tune of 90 percent. Everybody is on welfare in this country. The problem is that we all too often have socialism for the rich and rugged free enterprise capitalism for the poor. That's the problem." http://cityobservatory.org/dr-king-socialism-for-the-rich-and-rugged-free-enterprise-capitalism-for-the-poor. Accessed August 1, 2020.

177 Given the undeniability of the unsustainability data, it should not be surprising that a new concept has appeared on the scene: sustainable capitalism. Personally, I don't know how this reborn capitalism is capitalism at all. It requires, for example, forfeiture of the profit motive, regulated executive pay (aligned to sustainable long-term objectives), eliminating quarterly reporting, GDP goals adjusted radically downwards, eliminating the myopic focus on "the bottom line" and replacing it with a robust principle of sustainability beginning in business school, and so forth. The reader might want to investigate and form his or her own opinion. On one side is economist Michael Munger, who argues a version of Margaret Thatcher's TINA: "Unless you are willing to advocate monarchism, or actual communist dictatorship, markets and democracy are the only two mechanisms we have for organizing society." (https://www.moralmarkets.org/book/is-capitalism-sustainable) See his brief account "Is Capitalism Sustainable?" *American Institute for Economic Research*. https://www.aier.org/article/is-capitalism-sustainable. On the other side, Yvon Chouinard, the founder of the outdoor apparel company

alternative plane proposed by anarchists, it will be useful to consider anarchism's specific objection to government and the state. We can do so briefly by analyzing a pointed and quite colorful mock-Biblical admonishment to his readers from Pierre-Joseph Proudhon.

> Thou shalt respect thy representatives and functionaries whom the fortune of the ballot or the good pleasure of the State has given thee.
>
> Thou shalt obey the laws which their wisdom has given thee.
>
> Thou shalt pay thy taxes faithfully.
>
> And thou shalt love the Government, thy lord and thy god, with all thy heart, with all thy soul, and with all thy mind, because the Government knows better than thou what thou art, what thou art worth, and what is good for thee; and it has the power to chastise those who disobey its commandments, as well as to recompense to the fourth generation those who are agreeable to it...
>
> To be governed is to be kept in sight, inspected, spied upon, directed, law-driven, numbered, enrolled, indoctrinated, preached at, controlled, estimated, valued, censured, commanded, by creatures who have neither the right, nor the wisdom, nor the virtue to do so...To be governed is to be at every operation, at every transaction, noted, registered, enrolled, taxed, stamped, measured, numbered, assessed, licensed, authorized, admonished, forbidden, reformed, corrected, punished. It is, under the pretext of

---

Patagonia, says, "I believe the accepted model of capitalism that demands endless growth deserves the blame for the destruction of nature, and it should be displaced." See his interview, "No Such Thing as Sustainability," *Fast Company*, http://www.fastcompany.com/1298102/patagonias-founder-on-why-theres-no-such-thing-as-sustainability. Accessed August 8, 2020.

> public utility, and in the name of the general interest, to be placed under contribution, trained, ransomed, exploited, monopolized, extorted, squeezed, mystified, robbed; then, at the slightest resistance, the first word of complaint, to be repressed, fined, despised, harassed, tracked, abused, clubbed, disarmed, choked, imprisoned, judged, condemned, shot, deported, sacrificed, sold, betrayed; and, to crown all, mocked, ridiculed, outraged, dishonored. That is government; that is its justice; that is its morality. And to think that there are democrats among us who pretend that there is any good in government.[178]

Proudhon's diatribe arguably contains the essential features of any self-respecting anarchist critique of the government-state. The first point to note is that in classical anarchist writing these two entities are generally collapsed into one, and typically termed "government." The next feature to note is the pervasiveness of violence in Proudhon's statement. This is no accident. Anarchists argue that the state is ultimately unjustifiable—hence, impractical—because it is saturated by one essential quality: violence. Indeed, a widely accepted definition of "the state" is *that entity which has a monopoly on violence.* None other than the eminently staid German sociologist Max Weber (1864–1920) verifies this contention: "Ultimately, one can define the modern state sociologically only in terms of the specific means peculiar to it, as to every political association, namely, the use of physical force." He continues:

> "Every state is founded on force," said Trotsky at Brest-Litovsk. That is indeed right. If no social institutions existed which knew the use of violence, then the concept of "state" would be eliminated, and a condition would emerge

178 Pierre-Joseph Proudhon, *The General Idea of the Revolution in the 19th Century*, Epilogue, 1851, *Anarchist Library*, https://theanarchistlibrary.org/library/pierre-joseph-proudhon-the-general-idea-of-the-revolution-in-the-19th-century. Accessed August 9, 2020.

> that could be designated as "anarchy," in the specific sense of this word. Of course, force is certainly not the normal or the only means of the state—nobody says that—but force is a means specific to the state. Today the relation between the state and violence is an especially intimate one... Today, we have to say that a state is a human community that (successfully) claims the monopoly of the legitimate use of physical force within a given territory.[179]

Is Weber suggesting that if the institutional infrastructure for state violence were dismantled, the formation that I am advocating in this manifesto, namely anarchism, would likely, if not inevitably, "emerge"? How should we understand Weber's phrase "'anarchy, in the specific sense of this word"? I hope the reader will agree that this remarkable assertion from such an influential rationalist defender of order, authority, force, patriarchy, and class privilege is worth a brief digression. The conclusion may be surprising.

Weber was intimately familiar with the anti-statist arguments of anarchism. In the spring of 1913 and again in 1914, he lived at "the enchanted and eroticized mountain of Belle Époque Europe,"[180] the Swiss village of Ascona on Monte Verità. This was the location of a utopian counter-culture community of social rebels advocating such antinomian ideas as sexual liberation, proto-feminism, neo-paganism, dietary purification, and radical politics. Otto Gross (1877–1920), a leading figure at Ascona, was an avid student of Peter Kropotkin's social anarchist theories as well as Leo Tolstoy's more individualist ethical anarchism. In fact, Kropotkin himself had visited Ascona, as had two other, more fiery, anarchists mentioned earlier, Mikhail Bakunin and Errico Malatesta. Gross, a pioneering psychoanalyst, held that Freud's theory of repression as the price to be paid for

179 Max Weber, "Politics as Vocation," lecture manuscript, p. 1, https://tinyurl.com/y3cns8u8. Accessed August 10, 2020.

180 Y. B. Kuiper, "Tolstoyans on a Mountain: From New Practices of Asceticism to the Deconstruction of the Myths of Monte Verità," *Journal of Religion in Europe* 6 (2013): 6.

civilization was as dangerous as it was wrong. Instead, Gross advocated for a "new eroticism." Positing an integral relationship between desire and politics, this view held that relaxed sexual mores would have the effect of defusing the ticking timebomb of individual, relational, and societal violence resulting from repression. Why would a well-respected bourgeois German professor spend his Easter holidays in such a "wild zone"?[181] The most likely explanation is that on the eve of World War I, Weber, the inveterate student of emergent social trends, clearly discerned the coming cataclysm wrought by the perfected yet "petrified" rationalism of Enlightenment Europe. His "fascination" with anarchism, as one scholar puts it, may have derived from what he saw as anarchism's "critical potential" to create a subject, a citizen, capable of resisting the "dehumanizing, irrational" explosion of state violence lying in murderous wait just around the corner. Beyond that particular disaster, Weber "was not indifferent to Gross's notion of the energy—sexual, political—that the 'resistant' individual bursts with and directs against the assimilating pressure of the state."[182] Anarchism, Weber seems to have thought, just might offer effective tools for a more just and humane society. This most practical of sociologists, in other words, saw a promising practicality in "'anarchy,' in the specific sense of the word."

Proudhon's canonical statement certainly resounds with Weber's characterization of violence as the defining feature and function of the state. He, like all anarchists, however, would vehemently reject Weber's contention that this violence is "legitimate." That is, its

---

181 Wild, at least, to Weber's milieu of "respectable" society. Shortly before Weber's visit, the *Winterthur Tageblatt* laments "the unwelcome appearance [in Ascona] of ambassadors of German metropolitan anarchism, syndicalist wandering preachers [i.e., advocates of anarchist trade unions], and emancipated females. They have been shown to be representatives of acute metropolitan sickness, of sexual perversion, and of homosexual prostitution." In Whimster, *Max Weber*, 8-9.

182 Christian Moraru, *The D.H. Lawrence Review* 30, no. 1 (2001): 74–75. I also referred to Douglas Brent McBride, *German Studies Review* 23, no. 3 (2000): 607–08, and the book of which these two references are reviews, Sam Whimster, *Max Weber and the Culture of Anarchy* (London: Palgrave MacMillan, 1999).

legitimacy is dependent on nothing but *its own* proclamations of legitimacy. Such proclamations are enshrined in the vast infrastructure of constitutions, decrees, laws, and courts that the state in its "wisdom" has given us for our own good, and, just in case we object, backed with the perpetual threat of violence from the police, the military, and the prison-industrial complex. If the "plane of justification" on which the state establishes itself can be shown to be nothing but an obvious publicly-accepted specter, somewhat akin to the diamond engagement ring, the carceral threat to life and limb to anyone who challenges it is undeniably real. Thus, in the anarchist analysis, it is solely the state's iron-grip monopoly on violence that explains its perpetuation. The fact that this threat of violence is at the heart of the capitalist-government-state triumvirate produces the further denunciations expressed or intimated in Proudhon's statement: economic exploitation, classism, greed, conformist repression, corruption, immorality, domination, and a deleterious effect on human relations.

Yes, anarchism is an impractical way of thinking and being—*on the current plane*. If the reader thinks that my argument thus far has any merit, however, that is not the end of the matter. A next step follows; namely, to genuinely pose the question with which we began this section: "What is the good of passing from one untenable position to another, of seeking justification always on the same plane?" This is not intended as a hypothetical question seeking a merely theoretical solution. It may appear so at the macro level of our multi-trillion-dollar capitalist economy coupled with the constitutional government and violent nation state that prop it up. Like Žižek/Jameson, you might agree that "it is easier to imagine an end to the world than an end to capitalism," or even with Thatcher that "there is no alternative" to the current system. In what follows, I hope to convert you at least to the degree of Ursula Le Guin's faith that although the power of the status quo appears as inevitable and inescapable as the divine right of kings once did, "any human power can be resisted and changed by human beings." I agree with Le Guin that "resistance and change often begin in art" because art has proven repeatedly to stimulate the imagination, and sometimes even provide models, regarding viable alternatives to the status quo. "To begin," of course, implies that there is more to come. What would an anarchist recommend as a next step? Recall the Marxist concept of praxis mentioned earlier. I suggested that praxis is a way of intermixing two modes typically held apart: speculative theorizing and concrete action. In praxis, theorizing *is* a real-world activity; it is *already* a way of acting in and *on* the world, as Le Guin claims for art-making. The essential next move is to transmute the object of theoretical contemplation, as Marx says, into a "*sensuous human activity, practice.*" This is a move to "subjectively" embody and enact the objectively contemplated idea. This is all to say that because "all social life is essentially practical," we have no recourse but to "prove the truth" of the practicality of anarchist values *in practice*.

Historically, anarchists have recommended as genuine praxis revolution, insurrection, industrial sabotage, ecotage, general strikes, civil disobedience, and direct action. At the other extreme, they have recommended small utopian communities, temporary autonomous zones, hacktivism, squatting, occupation, and individualist retreat from society. I feel confident that none of these options will appeal to my readers—they are too impractical within the current context of your life. So, I would like to suggest an option that is undeniably practical. In and of itself, the anarchist suggestion is as sane and staid as the most bourgeois liberalism. So much so as to make manifest "the strange phenomenon of the *opposition* to Anarchism."[183] The fact that it was "Red" Emma Goldman (1869–1940), "the most dangerous woman in America," in FBI director J. Edgar Hoover's estimation, who said that, adds a certain crucial twist to anarchism's saneness. It is practical, sane, and staid *not* in the reformist spirit that liberalism demands of it. So, being, as we are, on the plane of the status quo, this is the point where

183 Emma Goldman, "Anarchism: What It Really Stands For," https://www.lib.berkeley.edu/goldman/pdfs/EmmaGoldman_ANARCHISM_WHATITREALLYSTANDSFOR.pdf. Accessed August 1, 2020. Emphasis added.

the "radicality" of anarchism will necessarily stick out for you. That is, anarchism is rooted in an approach that disavows the very premises of the capitalism-government-state system on which your current life is presumably (comfortably enough) situated. The only significant obstacle to practicality and practice that needs to be overcome is tripping on that rooty trail, and refusing even to try another path.

5.
How to Be an Anarchist

Yes, we are dreamers, because, like children, we don't like nightmares.
—Anarchist Federation[184]

Anarchism is a value system eschewing reliance on authority, and encouraging direct participation based on one's own intelligence and creativity. Obviously, such a system should have little tolerance for the *prescriptions* that a "how to" suggests. I would hope that even an experimental anarchist would be suspicious of preformulated rules about how to proceed. It is not really possible to say "how to be an anarchist" because anarchism so deeply values solutions forged in the heat of some presently given situation. Constructing solutions from within the situation also means, of course, that the strategies must be devised by the very people impacted by the situation. None of this can be prescribed.[185] As the quote above indicates, what makes a solution

184 Anarchist Federation, *Beyond Resistance: A Revolutionary Manifesto for the Millennium*, https://theanarchistlibrary.org/library/anarchist-federation-beyond-resistance-a-revolutionary-manifesto-for-the-millenium. Accessed July 23, 2020.

185 Anticipating the same demands for specifics in her auditors as I do my readers, Lucy Parsons (1853-1942), in a famous lecture titled *The Principles of Anarchism*, said: "Still unsatisfied perhaps, the inquirer [into anarchism] seeks for details, for ways and means, and whys and wherefores. How will we go on like human beings eating and sleeping, working and loving, exchanging and dealing, without government? So used have we become to 'organized authority' in every department of life that ordinarily we cannot conceive of the most common-place avocations being carried on without their interference and 'protection.' But anarchism is not compelled to outline a complete organisation of a free society. To do so with any assumption of authority would be to place another barrier in the way of coming generations. The best thought of today may

anarchist, as opposed to liberal or illiberal or conservative or communist or fascist, is the discernible presence of the basic values I have been naming, and will continue to name.

One practices anarchy by devising strategies to express its values. By turns, these strategies apply to the personal, the community, and the political spheres of society. Recall that I suggested earlier that we think of the micro-level as involving primarily *personal ethics*, the meso-level as being concerned primarily with *organizational modeling*, and the macro-level as operating as large scale *political agitation*. In truth, these three "levels" are highly porous. As the famous rallying cry of second wave feminists, *the personal is political,* insists, it is not possible to isolate these three interconnected spheres from one another.[186]

The image of a fractal is instructive here. Fractals are complex patterns that are identical across different scales. They appear in nature, in, for instance, the repeated self-similar patterns found in snowflakes, lightning bolts, trees, ocean waves, mountains, clouds, geographic terrains, seashells, craters, and DNA. So, for example, the patterning within the tiniest twigs of a tree resemble the patterning found within the large branches, which in turn resemble the patterning of the tree's trunk. Fractals also appear in mathematics, computers, shapes, art, law, and time itself.[187] This fact is suggestive of a certain "naturalness" to the fractal quality of society as well. We don't have to take this suggestion

---

become the useless vagary of tomorrow, and to crystallise it into a creed is to make it unwieldy." http://lucyparsons.org/the-principles-of-anarchism.php. *Lucy Parsons Center*. Accessed September 5, 2020.

186 Carol Hanisch, "The Personal is Political," http://www.carolhanisch.org/CHwritings/PIP.html. Accessed August 27, 2020. In a move that any anarchist would condone, neither Hanisch nor the several other women who were credited with the phrase has claimed authorship. The reason for this reluctance is that the phrase had been circulating in feminists groups for years before Hanisch's article appeared in 1969. Prominent feminist Gloria Steinem quipped that taking credit for the phrase would be like claiming "authorship" for World War II. See Kerry T. Burch, *Democratic Transformations: Eight Conflicts in the Negotiation of American Identity* (London: Continuum, 2012)

187 See *The Fractal Forge*, https://thefractalforge.com/what-is-a-fractal. Accessed August 26, 2020.

so far as to posit it as an inherent ontological feature of reality; we can simply apply it as a working hypothesis and consider that the patterns of the personal are found in the organizational, the organizational in the political, the political in the personal, and so on in every scale. Fusing *the personal is political* with our fractal metaphor, we might conclude that altering patterns in our personal lives is a profoundly direct attempt to *mutate* the pattern writ large as "the status quo." In this final section, I will present various strategies for anarchist action where I believe my readers are most apt to apply them: in the personal and organizational domains of their lives.

A crucial concept to bear in mind while reading is "the anarchic habit." In practicing these strategies, you will be developing this habit. The "fractal" assumption is, of course, that this habit is like a pattern that may extrapolate ever-farther outwards. In what follows, I hope you will discover for yourself the "anarchogenic,"[188] or expressions of the productive values that potentially seed a larger scale anarchism—cooperation, mutual support, direct participation, egalitarianism, decentralization, order; rejection of authoritarianism, domination, coercion, and institutionalized hierarchy. Once you have recognized that you, too, have the capacity for these dispositions (even if only as a temporary thought experiment) you can use anarchist strategies to form them into a lived habit.

It should prove fruitful to my reader if we consider these strategies not in terms of an ideology that must be accepted, but as elements to be applied in a life design. Designers often speak of their products in terms of a "solution" to a problem. Yet, somewhat philosophically, they quickly add that since the world is in constant flux, design must be "adaptive."[189] Our anarchist design is similar. This statement by Dilar Dirik, a sociologist and anarchist activist in the Kurdish women's

188 This neologism is an adaptation of one that anarchist scholar John Clark used in a private conversation with me to describe a similar phenomenon in the establishment of fascism: fasciogenic.

189 See, for instance, Jessica Lascar, "What is Product Design?" website, https://uxdesign.cc/what-is-product-design-d95cd5339f5c. Accessed September 26, 2020.

movement, captures several important points to bear in mind as we engage in this somewhat paradoxical exercise of "how to be an anarchist."

> Feminist prefigurative politics, less focused on measurable impact, or provable or testable formulas, but concerned with care, sustainability, collectivism, ecology, and the self-determination and autonomy of different identities, allows us a view of revolution that is different from a fatherlike radical politics that treats society as a group of objects to be disciplined and led. Revolutionary processes require patience and love, hope and belief.[190]

Dirik mentions "care, sustainability, collectivism, ecology, and the self-determination and autonomy of different identities." Negatively, she mentions values that are precisely *not* in play in an anarchist solution, such as being "focused on measurable impact, or provable or testable formulas." With this point, we arrive at a feature of this "how to" that readers may find disappointing or frustrating. "Ready-made solutions," Dirik observes, "are an expression of a capitalist mode of thought, which demands instant gratification without labor, care, and sustainability."[191] Refusing to pass from one untenable position to another, refusing to seek justification always on the same plane, a section titled "how to be an anarchist" must tread a fine line between saying too much (thereby becoming "fatherlike," rigidly overdetermining) and saying too little (thereby becoming evasive and unhelpful).

The approach to lived anarchism in terms of design elements provides an important clue about how to hold what follows. Elements are ingredients, materials, bits and pieces, principles, aspects. As opposed to the predetermined "group of objects" assumed by leaders who have

190 Dilar Dirik, "'Only with You, This Broom Will Fly:' Rojava, Magic, and Sweeping Away the State Inside Us," in Cindy Milstein, ed., *Deciding for Ourselves: The Promise of Direct Democracy* (Chico: AK Press, 2020), 254.
191 Dirik, "'Only with You," 253.

already decided on the direction of a solution,[192] anarchist elements must be applied and assembled by all those impacted. Doing so requires "patience and love, hope and belief" precisely because of the precarity that follows from our refusal to take refuge in the status quo. Who can say in advance what will emerge out of *your own ideas* about how to implement the values that we are calling anarchist? I will begin with more abstract elements and move toward more concrete ones.

UTOPIA

With the word "utopia" I expect to raise eyebrows at the outset. I also aim to address head on the most popular disclaimer of anarchism from the mid-nineteenth century to the present day—it is utopian! If you are going to be an anarchist, I believe you will need to embrace the concept of utopia as a kind of *leitmotiv*, or recurring salient theme in your thinking. I encourage the reader to consider what I call the *utopian hypothesis*. Generally, this hypothesis holds that it is possible to create a world where human, animal, and environmental harmony and wellbeing are optimized. If "world" is too broad a category for you to imagine real-life applications of these qualities, ask yourself what in *your world*—an office, say, or a church or yoga community, might look like when organized by mutual support, egalitarianism, decentralization, direct participation in decision-making, and so forth. We already know what such places look like when *devoid* of these values. They are dominated by centralized top-down authority, which generates a hierarchical structure, which automatically disables shared input to workplace decisions, which stifles creativity and enthusiasm, which

---

192 Dirik's comment about "fatherlike radical politics" appears to be a reference to the Marxist side of socialist thought, which anarchists refer to as "authoritarian socialism." It is, of course, also statist. A further "fatherlike" fault of Marxism is its insistence on the necessity of *vanguardism*. This approach assumes that only some elite group of people, such as intellectuals and book writers, is capable of formulating the revolutionary strategy for everyone else to follow. My refusal to provide prescriptive examples is based on my agreement with the anarchist critique of vanguardism.

spawns maladaptive human relationships, which damages employee morale, which validates the need for an even more dominant authority, and so on and so forth. The utopian hypothesis is an element in *thought*. It enables the specifically anarchist praxis-oriented speculative theorizing that potentially leads to concrete action. To consider the stakes of the utopian hypothesis all we need to do is imagine—to look at!—what its denial entails.

If you want to experiment with anarchist ways of being, I believe that it is crucial not only that the eternally maligned notion of "utopia" circulates robustly in your thinking (about relationships, about organizational life, etc.), but that it retains its *aura* while doing so. I am using aura in the ancient sense of an "ambience" or "atmosphere" that appears to accompany an object, "charging" it with authenticity and efficacy. This idea itself is charged with potential misunderstanding. In contrast to the New Age idea of aura that posits the literal actuality of an energy field or subtle body around an object, this sense recognizes that it is *we* who create the charged "breeze" of an aura.[193] This imputation makes it no less real. For, in doing so we maintain a direct, immediate relation to the object. The value of this concept is not as a mere idea to be consumed. Like genuine art, it bears the promise of a favorable condition that society in its present form does not allow; and if such an idea, like such art, resists understanding, this is only because it confronts the beholder with its own impossible demands. The aura is a sign of this utopian promise. The aura must be preserved. "One cannot abolish it," Theodor Adorno insists, "and still want art." One cannot abolish the aura surrounding the idea of utopia and still want the conditions for actual utopian circumstances. To paraphrase, Adorno: Aura is not only the here and now of the utopian hypothesis; it is whatever goes beyond its actual, lived content. We cannot abolish the aura of "utopia" and still want an optimally congenial situation.[194]

193 The Latin original, *aura*, means "a breeze, a breath of air, the air,' from ancient Greek *aúra*, "breeze, soft wind," from *aḗr*, "air." See *Wiktionary*, https://en.wiktionary.org/wiki/aura. Accessed August 28, 2020.

194 Theodor Adorno, *Aesthetic Theory*, trans., Robert Hullot-Kentor (Minneapolis:

An anarchist, I believe, is well served by keeping the charged atmosphere of *utopia* always present in mind. When considering a personal or work relationship, for instance, when contemplating one's situation with colleagues, when thinking about how to organize a multi-person project, when interacting with family members or a group of friends, an anarchist is someone who infuses anarchist values into the situation. The contemporary anarchist slogan *a better world is possible* says as much. A better personal relationship is possible. A better work environment is possible. A better organization is possible. What would make them better is, initially, the elimination of coercive authority, the dismantling of unjustified hierarchy, the cancelation of the capitalist insistence on exploitative exchange, and all of the rest, and, then, actualization of cooperative support, dialogical decision-making, and exchange based not on profit but mutual desire to enhance one another's creativity and intelligence.

Jonathon Feldman acerbically opines that "Basically, if you're not a utopianist, you're a schmuck."[195] Harsh, yes; but I think Emma Goldman expresses a similar sentiment when she marvels at "the strange phenomenon of the *opposition* to Anarchism." Can you think of any truly justifiable, indeed *humane*, reasons to oppose, in your own life, the moment-to-moment drive toward anarchist utopia? After briefly introducing the concept of "concrete utopia," I will give examples of anarchist utopian design.

CONCRETE UTOPIA

Despite the brutalist Soviet-era images it evokes, the term "concrete utopia" has nothing to do with architecture.[196] Rather, it names an

University of Minnesota Press, 1997), 45. The original reads: "Aura is not only—as [Walter] Benjamin claimed—the here and now of the artwork, it is whatever goes beyond its factual givenness, its content; one cannot abolish it and still want art."

195 Cited in David Graeber, *Fragments of an Anarchist Anthropology* (Chicago: Prickly Paradigm Press, 2004), epigraph.

196 Or does it? See the MoMA exhibit "Toward a Concrete Utopia: Architecture in

organizational *process*. It makes an intentional play on the term from which "concrete," the Latin *concrescere*, "to grow together," originates. As the standard connotation of concrete as *solid, actual, real* indicates, concrete utopia signifies a *material* growth, or a growth with and out of our present material conditions. For this reason, it is to be distinguished from the idealized utopias found in literature, beginning with Thomas More's *Utopia*. Wanting to preserve and honor Ursula Le Guin's insistence that imaginative art can have effects in the real world, we might view concrete utopia as *the next step*, the praxis that comes after Le Guin's "imagination," Marx's "contemplation," or indeed, our own "utopian hypothesis."

The concept of "concrete utopia" originated with the Marxist thinker Ernst Bloch (1885–1977). But Bloch was, I believe, sufficiently heretical for us to claim his concept as our own. (He was expelled from his East German university position for his interpretations of Marx.) The title of his eccentric, majestic, somewhat apocalyptic three-volume book provides a clue as to the aim of a concrete utopia: *The Principle of Hope*. "It is a question of learning hope," Bloch begins. Significant for our purposes, hope is not a spontaneous emotional quality; it is a *condition* that must be *learned*. We are, again, in the domain of praxis, of doing, acting, forming, creating. Similar to many ideas we have encountered in this book—Fisher's capitalist realism, Beckett's plane of justification, the vapor-like quality of the spectacle, etc.—Bloch argues that hope must be learned because our default mechanism is to act reflexively, unthinkingly in the world as mere spectators of the *What Is*. In a recurring theme in this manifesto, Bloch argues that the status quo blinds our imaginations to the *Not Yet*, to, that is, a possible creation adequate to our utopian hypothesis. This is the reason that hope, for Bloch, is not primarily an emotional affect, but rather a species of action, one which "requires people

---

Yugoslavia, 1948–1980," https://www.moma.org/calendar/exhibitions/3931?locale=en. Accessed September 4, 2020.

who throw themselves actively into what is becoming."[197] "Concrete utopia" is a dynamic practice that "*contains within it the forward surge of an achievement which can be anticipated*."[198] Consistent with the anarchist refusal to prescribe solutions, "can be anticipated" does not entail "will be achieved." In the examples that I will mention, the "failure" of many anarchist communities may, I believe, be ascribed to this confusion—a confusion that creates an even larger obstacle, I believe, for the *critics* of anarchist utopian experiments. So, to clarify, while "real utopia" assumes feasibility on the current plane of justification, "concrete utopia" refers to *practice*. In literally *practicing* within a utopian anarchist project, participants are simultaneously literally *making practicable/practical* the desired realization of a transformed communal formation.

ANARCHIST UTOPIAN DESIGNS

A document of efforts to implement anarchist utopias from the mid-nineteenth century to the present would be surprisingly extensive. It would showcase a myriad of social experiments ranging in size from housing co-ops; squats; do it yourself (DIY) initiatives; free schools; cooperative organizations and businesses; worker-run factories; communes; intentional communities; autonomous regions and municipalities; and mass societies. If we extended that list to include what David Graeber (1961-2020) calls "fragments of an anarchist anthropology," namely, the "alternative moralities" buried in the world's ethnographic record, the list would explode, quite possibly challenging a list of statist societies. In an instructive comment, Graeber reminds us that "The basic principles of anarchism—self-organization, voluntary association, mutual aid"—we should add direct social participation, decentralization, egalitarianism—"have been around about as long as humanity. The same goes for the rejection of the state and of all forms

197 Bloch, *Principle*, 148.
198 Bloch, *Principle*, 3.

of structural violence, inequality, or domination…even the assumption that all these forms are somehow related and reinforce each other."[199] Here, I will present fragments of an anarchist design highlighting some basic features of the kinds of communities mentioned above, including my own experiences with concrete utopia in the forms of the high school I attended and the educational cooperative I founded. Taken together, my aspiring anarchist readers should begin to discern the potential lineaments of their own unique designs.

Housing Collectives

The online magazine of the U.S. government's Department of Housing and Urban Development (HUD) has a page titled "Homeownership: The American Dream." It unabashedly states that "For many Americans, owning a home is an essential part of the American dream that conveys a number of economic benefits, such as the ability to accumulate wealth and access credit by building home equity, reduce housing costs through the mortgage interest deduction, and gain long-term savings over the cost of renting." HUD's goal is thus "to ensure that the opportunity to seize this part of the American Dream is available to as many Americans as possible."[200] I say "unabashedly" for two reasons. First, recall that HUD's lax regulation of bank mortgages, in service to the American Dream, played a leading role in the 2008 international financial collapse. In the spirit of the crony capitalism that I discussed earlier, the obligations of financial institutions to shareholders and politicians have created a situation in which their "missions require them to distort markets."[201] The second reason is that this imperative

---

199 Graeber, "Fragments," 2.

200 *Edge: an online magazine*, https://www.huduser.gov/portal/pdredge/pdr-edge-frm-asst-sec-081318.html. Accessed September 25, 2020.

201 Lawrence H. White, "Housing Finance and the 2008 Financial Crisis," *Downsizing the Federal Government*, https://www.downsizinggovernment.org/hud/housing-finance-2008-financial-crisis. Accessed September 25, 2020. Democrats and Republicans in America reinforce this ideology through federal tax policy, which "gives special preferences to owner-occupied housing, through the mortgage interest deduction and capital gains exclusion. Local land use policies allow single-family homes to be built

to own a house is grounded in nothing but capitalist propaganda.[202] As Brookings fellow Jenny Schuetz puts it, "Stable, decent housing in a safe, healthy community is a fundamental need. Owning one's home is not."[203]

In the United States, housing collectives (or cooperatives) have been an alternative to individual home ownership since the 1920s. The earliest co-ops in Europe date to the mid-nineteenth century.[204] As can be expected, the spirit in which a co-op is organized depends on the values of the members. As can further be expected, most co-ops tout advantages concerning taxation, rates of return, lower cost per square foot, resell values, and so on.

Anarchist co-ops, by contrast, emphasize community participation. One such co-op was in the news recently for outbidding a land developer who wanted to buy the adjacent lots to build apartment buildings.[205] That co-op was Trumbullplex, an anarchist housing cooperative in Detroit. Its main space consist in two Victorian-era houses with a performance and art space, as well as outdoor greenspaces and a vegetable garden. Members split the monthly mortgage payments along agreed-on equitable lines. Household duties are divided into four areas: maintenance, long-term repair, finance, and outreach. Members meet weekly to discuss issues, conflicts, and immediate needs, and to assign tasks within the four areas. From the current schedule, there

---

in more locations, and with fewer barriers, than apartment buildings. Political rhetoric, again from both parties, reinforces the idea that renting a home should be seen as a temporary state, a waystation on the journey to the final destination of homeownership," Jenny Schuetz, "Renting the American Dream: Why homeownership shouldn't be a prerequisite for middle-class financial security," https://tinyurl.com/yxputkjd. Accessed September 25, 2020.

202 See "How Are Capitalism and Private Property Related?" *Investopedia*, https://tinyurl.com/yy9vas3m. Accessed September 25, 2020.

203 Jenny Schuetz, "Renting the American Dream." Accessed September 25, 2020.

204 For a brief history of housing cooperatives, see Gerald Sazama, "A Brief History of Affordable Housing Cooperatives in the United States," *UConn Library: Economic Working Papers*, https://tinyurl.com/y42rma52. Accessed September 25, 2020.

205 See "Detroit sides with anarchists over developer in land bid," *Detroit Free Press*, https://tinyurl.com/y6jd6hte. Accessed September 25, 2020.

also appears to be a robust cultural program, consisting largely of youth-oriented underground music.[206]

If living together under such conditions sounds rather mundane, recall the principles of prefiguration, praxis, and concrete utopia. These potent principles are activated only within lived situations, no matter how minimal or everyday. As someone who has interacted with them since the late 1970s, I can confidently offer my view that the members of such housing co-ops are well aware of anarchism's larger goal of social transformation. Living in this manner, co-op members are active agents manifesting the changes they desire to see in society at large—equality, mutual support, transparency, cooperative decision-making, self-management, and so on. In the spirit of concrete utopia, they are *surging forward* on a more tenable plane, doing, acting, forming, and creating within the commonplace scope of living together.

I can understand that, my advocacy notwithstanding, this result might strike the reader as trivial and inconsequential. So, I will try to bolster it with an example from my own experience.

Free Schools

"Well, that's pretty much what the schools are like, I think: they reward discipline and obedience, and they punish independence of mind."[207] That's anarchist social critic and emeritus MIT linguistics professor Noam Chomsky on the nature of schooling in America. In my own experience, his assertion is irrefutable. My agreement stems not only from how I was personally affected by schooling from kindergarten to the Ph.D., but my observations of how my fellow classmates, friends, and siblings were impacted as well. The strange thing about Chomsky's assertion is that it is wholly uncontroversial: I believe that you will agree with the claim whether you view it as pointing to a social ailment or to a social benefit. If you agree with Chomsky that

---

206 Trumbullplex, https://trumbullplex.org. Accessed September 25, 2020.

207 Noam Chomsky, *Understanding Power* (New York: The New Press, 2002), 236.

"The highest goal in life is to inquire and create," and that, moreover, "The purpose of education from that point of view is just to help people to learn on their own," then you will readily agree with the assertion as indicating a negative feature of schooling.[208] If you think that schooling should function as what Louis Althusser calls an "ideological state apparatus"—an institution, that is, for the formation of well-behaved, subservient, and conformist citizens—then you will agree with the assertion as indicating a positive feature of schooling.[209] In fact, we can view a school as a concrete utopia or dystopia (depending on your view) in that it is the place where, from early childhood to adulthood, we are formed into agents who replicate societal norms and values. In Althusser's term, we are "interpellated" into the capitalist-governance-state apparatus that was discussed earlier. In Althusser's critique of ideology, "interpellation" means *called, hailed, brought into being, given identity* as a subject of a particular social formation. If you want to muffle this call for yourself or for your children, what can you do? If you desire to add another layer of resistance to getting stuck in the ruts of *the same plane,* what can you do? One anarchist solution is: free school.

It should not be surprising that anarchism highly values education. Tending, as they typically do, to eschew an essentialist view of human nature, anarchists believe that whether we become competitive or cooperative individuals, say, is largely a matter of education. As philosopher and scholar of education Judith Suissa puts it, "the question of 'what should our society be like' is, for the anarchist...logically prior to any questions about what kind of education we want."[210] The reason for this priority lies in the inherently, though often obscured, political

---

208 Emphasis added. https://darwinessay.net/discussions-education-noam-chomsky. Accessed September 28, 2020.

209 See Louis Althusser, "Ideology and Ideological State Apparatuses," *Marxist Archive*, https://www.marxists.org/reference/archive/althusser/1970/ideology.htm. Accessed September 28, 2020.

210 Judith Suissa, *Anarchism and Education: A Philosophical Perspective* (London: PM Press, 2010), 5.

nature of education. Questions concerning what should be taught, to and by whom, and toward what end, are *not*, in the first instance, pedagogical: they are political.

> The question for the philosopher of education, then, becomes threefold: One, what kind of society do we want? Two, what would education look like in this ideal society? And three, what kind of educational activities can best help to further the realization of this society?[211]

Such questions, of course, are posed in the spirit of prefiguration and concrete utopia. In this sense, they possess the spirit of the original anarchist school—Francisco Ferrer's (1859–1909) Escuela Moderna, or Modern School in Spain from 1901–1906. The Modern School, like all subsequent anarchist schools, operated as "an oasis from authoritarian control and as a means of passing on the knowledge to be free."[212]

If the idea of anarchist schools seems incredible, note that the directory of democratic education of the Alternative Education Resources Organization (AERO) alone list some two hundred schools dispersed throughout nearly fifty countries. And while most of these schools and educational organizations do not explicitly state that they are anarchist, we should recall the motto that "Anarchism is democracy taken seriously." This explanation on the AERO site is certainly indicative of the spirit we encountered in Chomsky's and Suissa's remarks.

> There is no monolithic definition of democratic education or democratic schools. But what we mean here is: education in which young people have the freedom to organize

211 Suissa, *Anarchism and Education*, 5.

212 See Ferrer's "The Origin and Ideals of the Modern School," https://theanarchistlibrary.org/library/francisco-ferrer-the-origin-and-ideals-of-the-modern-school. Accessed October 1, 2020. It should not surprise the reader by now that "a proponent of rationalist, secular education that emphasized reason, dignity, self-reliance, and scientific observation, as opposed to the ecclesiastical and dogmatic standard Spanish curriculum of the period" was executed as the leader of an insurrection against the state. (https://en.wikipedia.org/wiki/Ferrer_movement.)

> their daily activities, and in which there is equality and democratic decision-making among young people and adults.

In my own experience with a free school, "democratic education" was code for "anarchist education." (Surely, by now, the reader can forgive such public equivocation.) I would like to say more about that experience. My hope is to convey something of the significance, consequentiality, and far-reaching ramifications of even the smallest "sample" of direct encounter with anarchist values.

I attended a democratic/free/anarchist high school near Philadelphia in the 1970s. Although the experience lasted little more than a year, I feel that this experience forms the core of my life. It informs my way of relating to other people, individually and in community, my way of teaching, writing, thinking, and being. It informs my attitude toward politics, society, culture, and the world. And it colors my convictions concerning a possible "better world." When I say "school," don't picture a sprawling complex of fortified concrete buildings, parking lots, and athletic fields that is the typical American suburban high school. Rather, picture an old brick and wood-framed house on the grounds of an even older Catholic church. We were, after all, only twenty-one students at our peak (I was the fifteenth). It was cozy, if somewhat rundown. The living room was just that, a living room, with stuffed chairs and a couch and a sofa table strewn with magazines, books, coffee mugs, an ashtray, and various paraphernalia. The kitchen was a warm space where we made coffee and tea and sandwiches. Only the upstairs bedrooms were converted into anything school-like. In each, on what would now be called "distressed" hardwood floors, were a few mismatched rickety wooden chairs, and something like a blackboard. The first question I was asked when I entered this place was, "well, what do you want to learn?" For, our school had no mandated curriculum. Activities were driven by student curiosity and interest. There was no formal schedule, no age segregation, no rankings or power hierarchies. It was often difficult to tell the students from the teachers. There were no requirements or mandatory assignments. No schoolmaster ever meted out points and extra credit, deductions and demerits. We were never "rewarded" with grades. Just mature, honest face to face dialogue with each other at the end of each term to record our experience.[213] When conflicts arose, we sat down as a community and talked them through. When someone was in need, we helped. And we learned. My response to that initial question was, "Asian philosophy." A few days later, a youngish man named Bruce showed up to work with me. Bruce was not a teacher, much less an expert on Asian philosophy. He was "just" a member of the local community. Our school followed in the footsteps of anarchist Paul Goodman (1911–1972), who rightly insisted that, in free schools, "The use of certified teachers could be dispensed with and people like the druggist, the storekeeper, and the factory worker could be used as teachers."[214] Bruce suggested that we read through an ancient Buddhist text called the *Dhammapada*. Bruce had just recently dropped out of a manager training program at IBM. He had become alert to the broader social ramifications of his seemingly innocuous career choice. (IBM had been covertly involved in data analysis on the ground in the Vietnam War.) So, once a week, Bruce and I read through the verses of the *Dhammadpada*, discussing them with an eye to ways that "idealist spirituality" might impact "social materiality," and vice versa. He also gave me my first instructions in meditation. My first book after receiving tenure as a university professor

213 Concerned that I might be romanticizing the experience a bit in retrospect, I asked student #16, my older sister, Rosalie, what she remembered. Her email response: "I think that that school was very important for you. You were allowed to be the person you needed to be there. I think you needed little structure and were able to thrive as a viable human being—as you were, rather than as the Glenn who just refused to follow the rules."

214 Cited in Robert H. Haworth (ed.), *Anarchist Pedagogies: Collective Actions, Theories, and Critical Reflections on Education* (Oakland: PM Press, 2012), 130. Goodman's *Growing Up Absurd* became an important book for me at this time. Its subtitle may help explain its appeal to a struggling sixteen year old: *Problems of Youth in the Organized System.*

twenty-some years later was in honor of my teacher: a fresh translation of the *Dhammapada*, which I dedicated to Bruce. As anyone who knows my work can attest, the basic tension, or, in academic language, the problematic, of my subsequent investigations was established in those meetings with Bruce.

It is not an exaggeration to say that my life is a testament to the far-reaching ramifications of being exposed to anarchist values.

Worker Cooperatives

Like housing collectives, worker cooperatives have been around since the Industrial Revolution. As you might expect, that timing is no coincidence. With the growth of industrial capitalism came the diminishment of independent family and community-based businesses. The competition of large manufacturing, moreover, forced previously independent artisans and craftsmen into what leftists were coming to call, after Marx, "wage slavery"—the total, seemingly non-negotiable and irreversible dependence of workers on the boss for their livelihood. As a member of the new class of businessmen called *capitalist*, it was this boss, in collusion with his cronies, who determined the terms of the workers' livelihood. Because of the capitalist dogma of *privileging profit over people*, the bosses' calculations invariably meant that workers "sold" their time for paltry wages, thus living perpetually under the threat of deprivation and starvation. In a text from the *Economic Manuscripts* subtitled "Early Critique of the Bourgeois-Liberal View of the 'Freedom' of the Labourer," Marx quotes Simon Linguet, an early observer of what would become a deeply entrenched pattern, pertaining, in fact, to the present day.

> It is the impossibility of living by any other means that compels our farm labourers to till the soil whose fruits they will not eat, and our masons to construct buildings in which they will not live. It is want that drags them to those markets where they await masters who will do them

> the kindness of buying them. *It is want that compels them to go down on their knees to the rich man in order to get from him permission to enrich him.*[215]

The "want" referred to here is, in the emerging socialist analysis, created by the very logic of the market-government-state nexus that I discussed earlier. In short, as Marx again quotes Linguet, "The spirit of the law is property." Thus, Marx comments: "Stripped of the conditions of production, labourers are compelled by need to labour to increase the wealth of others in order themselves to live."

I would like to draw the reader's attention to two points. The first point is that the co-emergence of capitalism and its socialist critique is highly significant for our exploration of anarchism. While the Marxist version of that critique placed a special emphasis on the role that the working class would play in the revolution, anarchists tended to view our situation as workers as yet one more oppressive, and predictable, manifestation of the collusion between capitalism, government, and the state. Given the fact, however, that all but the wealthiest among us have to earn a living through our own labor, the issue of the workers' plight was front and center from the outset of anarchist social engagement. We have seen several robust examples of this involvement already, such as the events that led up to the Haymarket Massacre ("a chance to wipe out the leadership of the city's radical labor movement and send a message to all who would seek just wages, decent working conditions, and reduced hours for working men and women"), the trial of August Vaillant ("I have seen capital come, like a vampire, to suck the last drop of blood of" the workers), and the Industrial Workers of the World (founded on the principle that "The working class and the employing class have nothing in common."[216]). Indeed, as one observer notes, "As

215 https://www.marxists.org/archive/marx/works/1863/theories-surplus-value/ch07.htm. Accessed October 7, 2020.

216 This is the first sentence of the Preamble to the IWW North American Regional Administration Constitution. *IWW Resources*, https://iww.org/assets/iww-constitution.pdf. Accessed October 7, 2020.

we are beginning—but only beginning—to learn from scholars:"

> Anarchists played a fundamental role in launching a modern labor movement among key groups. Among German craftsmen of the 1880s, Jewish clothing workers of the 1890s, Italian clothing and garment workers of the 1910s, anarchist and syndicalist militants had an importance all out of proportion to their numbers. Without them craft and industrial unionism might not have happened for another generation. Certainly it would have lacked the verve, the dynamic impulse toward universality, the poetic spirit they imparted.[217]

Earlier, I characterized anarchism as "ungrand." I think that a central reason for this quality stems from anarchism's deep entanglement with, and struggle against, the effects of capitalism on our everyday lives. If, with my banal examples of anarchism in action—at home, in school, and now at work—readers are beginning to lose sight of the overwrought, highly dramatic caricature of the anarchism of "the street," then we are making progress!

My second point is that it is precisely the exploitation of labor from the Industrial Revolution down to the current Information Revolution that has stimulated the rise of worker cooperatives. Although "precariat" has replaced "proletariat" as the term for working people,[218] and although the service industry plays the economic role that heavy industry once did, the reality for workers is little changed. And "worker" no longer merely indicates "the working class" or "blue collar." Everyone who has to earn a living from their own labor is a worker. If you own an apartment building and collect rent from the tenants, you are not a

---

217 Paul Buhle, "Anarchism and American Labor," *International Labor and Working Class History*, Number 23, Spring 1983: 21.

218 Other recent telling terms for work today: bullshit job, McJob, gig worker, Uberfication of work, permatemp, zero-hour contract, workforce casualization, working poor, contingent work, day labor, dead-end job, even temporary executive and, in higher education, adjunctification.

worker: *they* are workers who pay *you* from their earnings. Whether you believe, as an increasing number of people do, that "landlords are social parasites...buy-to-let vampires...setting social inequality in stone," it is difficult to make a case that landlords *earn* their incomes.[219] If you own a company and derive your income largely from the profits generated from the labor of your employees, you are not a worker. Jeff Bezos did not "earn" $181 billion at Amazon, his wage workers did. Bezos does not, every single tick of the second hand, earn $2,219, double what the median U.S. worker makes in one week. No, he *takes* it, *appropriates* it, in Marxist language.[220] Bezos and others like him do so because the rules that have been put in place by the capitalism-government-state system make it permissible and legal, and, even perversely justifiable, to do so. If you are the CEO of a corporation where the board of directors pays your salary and bonuses based on profits earned by stock shares sold, you are not a worker. You work, but you are not a worker. The security of your position may be dependent on profits earned, but the security of your life, and the lives of your loved ones, is not. Even if you lose your job, surely, your $21.3 million per year payout plus lavish benefits package will allow you to endure the setback.[221] Marx's definition of the proletariat is not so far off today after all. He famously defined workers as those among us who are compelled to sell their "labor power" for wages (or salary) because we do not own the "means of production," i.e., the equipment and infrastructure required to

---

219 Rhik Samadder, "Landlords are social parasites," *The Guardian*, https://www.theguardian.com/commentisfree/2018/apr/16/landlords-social-parasites-last-people-should-be-honouring-buy-to-let. Accessed October 11, 2020.

220 See, "Jeff Bezos has gotten $70 billion richer in the past 12 months," *Business Insider*, https://www.businessinsider.com/how-rich-is-jeff-bezos-mind-blowing-facts-net-worth-2019-4. Accessed October 9, 2020.

221 This is the average payout—"using a 'realized' measure of CEO pay that counts stock awards when vested and stock options when cashed in rather than when granted"—for a CEO of one of the top 350 U.S. firms. See, Lawrence Mishel and Jori Kandra, "CEOs now earn 320 times as much as a typical worker," *Economic Policy Institute*, https://www.epi.org/publication/ceo-compensation-surged-14-in-2019-to-21-3-million-ceos-now-earn-320-times-as-much-as-a-typical-worker. Accessed October 11, 2020.

generate wealth.[222] Enter the worker cooperative.

The purpose of the worker cooperative is precisely to reclaim total ownership of the wealth produced by our personal labor. Typically, the spirit and strategies informing such cooperatives are, whether explicit or not, consistent with those of anarchism. For example, worker cooperatives are organized horizontally and democratically: one person, one vote. The vision, management, operations, policy, profits, etc., are shared among workers. No controlling board of directors. No bosses. Even the rather staid International Co-operative Alliance expresses these values with the typical "democratic" wink toward anarchism:

> Cooperatives are people-centred enterprises owned, controlled and run by and for their members to realise their common economic, social, and cultural needs and aspirations.
>
> Cooperatives bring people together in a democratic and equal way…[C]ooperatives are democratically managed by the "one member, one vote" rule. Members share equal voting rights regardless of the amount of capital they put into the enterprise.
>
> Cooperatives are based on the values of self-help, self-responsibility, democracy, equality, equity, and solidarity. In the tradition of their founders, cooperative members believe in the ethical values of honesty, openness, social responsibility, and caring for others.[223]

In contrast, perhaps, to housing and education, the large scale social and political ramifications of business cooperatives are easier to discern.

222 See the interesting article R. Jamil Jonna and John Bellamy Foster, "Marx's Theory of Working-Class Precariousness: Its Relevance Today," *Monthly Review*, https://monthlyreview.org/2016/04/01/marxs-theory-of-working-class-precariousness. Accessed October 8, 2020.

223 International Co-operative Alliance, https://www.ica.coop/en. Accessed October 9, 2020.

For instance, the Alliance alone represents over one billion individual people working for over three million cooperative businesses worldwide. According to the *World Cooperative Monitor*, in 2019 the top three hundred cooperative companies alone earned profits exceeding two trillion dollars.[224] Data shows that "Cooperatives contribute to the sustainable economic growth and stable, quality employment, employing 280 million people across the globe, in other words, 10% of the world's employed population." Indeed, it cannot be denied: "Cooperatives are not a marginal phenomenon."[225] Finally, in their study detailing the "key economic 'traps' of our times," including the "causes and mechanisms" of the 2007 global economic crisis, authors Claudia Sanchez Bajo and Bruno Roelants present a well-documented argument that cooperatives have not only avoided these traps—namely, consumption practices, liquidity capacity, and debt accumulation—indeed, have not merely thrived in an interminably volatile capitalist market, but have contributed to long-term stability within an international economy to which the cooperative sector, somewhat paradoxically, offers a radical alternative.[226] The authors also offer four case studies of large cooperatives. I can briefly highlight some features of these businesses to illustrate both the spirit and the viability of this approach.

The Natividad Island Divers' and Fishermen's Cooperative is the primary business entity on a small island of some four hundred residents off Baja California, in Mexico. The eighty-some worker-members dive

---

224 *World Cooperative Monitor*, https://monitor.coop/en. Accessed October 11, 2020.

225 International Co-operative Alliance, https://www.ica.coop/en. Accessed October 9, 2020.

226 Claudia Sanchez Bajo and Bruno Roelants, *Capital and the Debt Trap: Learning from Cooperatives in the Global Economy* (New York: Palgrave Macmillan, 2011), x. See also, "Are workers cooperatives the alternative to capitalism?," *International Socialist Review*. Although published in a Marxist journal, this article makes the anarchist critique that ultimately "Co–ops show that workers can run production, but they don't offer a strategy for changing society." It also offers a brief overview of the world's largest cooperative business, the Mondragón Cooperative Corporation, founded in Spain in 1956. https://isreview.org/issue/93/are-workers-cooperatives-alternative-capitalism. Accessed October 11, 2020.

mainly for abalones. In a country where the average monthly income is US$843,[227] divers can earn up to US$10,000 a month.[228]

Life on the island is austere, and the work is dangerous and difficult. Readers who are interested in a detailed account are encouraged to refer to the sources in the footnotes. They will find something short of an ideal solution in the account of this, and indeed to a certain extent of all, large cooperatives. Part of the reason for that shortfall has to do, of course, with the fact that regardless of their internal values these cooperatives must still operate, to a great extent, within the structures of capitalism. Nonetheless, in a time of environmental degradation the example of the Natividad Island cooperative "shows us how proper *democratic* control and management can ensure the preservation of the local environment."[229] Indeed, as with many of the anarchist and anarchist-oriented examples I have presented in this manifesto, the cooperative may well be offering value far beyond its immediate effects and scale.

> This story [of the Natividad Island Divers' and Fishermen's Cooperative] strengthens the argument of economics Nobel prize winner Elinor Ostrom in *Governing the Commons*, according to which natural resources are bound to be depleted if left under the sole management of businesses exclusively motivated by the short-term maximization of profit. Instead, they need to be managed under the joint control of the local inhabitants who have a stake in the maintenance of these resources.[230]

In the example of Ceralep Société Nouvelle, we see additional anarchist values at work, if not thus explicitly stated. The story of Ceralep, the primary French producer of large ceramic insulators since 1921, is one where fifty-some workers wrested control of a company from the

227 See, "Mexican households have an average of 3.8 members, $843 in monthly income," https://tinyurl.com/y4h2qs8j. Accessed October 19, 2020.

228 Bajo and Roelants, *Capital and the Debt Trap*, 130.

229 Bajo and Roelants, *Capital and the Debt Trap*, 134. Emphasis added.

230 Bajo and Roelants, *Capital and the Debt Trap*, 134.

destructive greed of absentee foreign companies. It is important to point out that in terms of the "rationality" of the global marketplace, the failure of Ceralep would have been a success, because *profitable,* to the American liquidation firm that took over operations in 2001. To the local community, not to mention the workers themselves, this "success" would have been devastating. Today, the cooperative is thriving, in large part due to the kinds of values that we see at work in explicitly anarchist projects.

> Transparency and circulation of information have improved as governance is more horizontal, allowing the Board members to take timely decisions. Minutes are not vertically imposed in advance onto the shareholders, who are now the worker–members of the cooperative. Control has been transferred from controllers at distance to present stakeholders who shoulder the risks.[231]

A major reason for success is, as one worker puts it, "we all spontaneously became our own bosses." Another worker expands on this central feature of any worker cooperative:

> Yes, we were working without a boss for the first time. It was just trusting each other. It was good to be involved, and we did all we could to make it work. But believing in it was not easy either, in the beginning. In the organization of the factory, now, people are more integrated, they feel more responsible to make things work. We don't need to wait until someone comes and tells us what to do, we know what we have to do. I always try to make an eleventh piece whereas before I used to make ten, not one more.

Significantly, to our purposes, all of this was predicated on a display of deep commitment by the workers and the local community. To begin the process of moving from corporate liquidation to worker's

---

231 Bajo and Roelants, *Capital and the Debt Trap*, 151.

cooperative, an initial €100,000 was required. I will let the workers speak for themselves.

> We met the workers with a megaphone in front of the factory, and explained to them that they had to find €100,000 within one or two days. They went home, looked at their savings, spoke with their families. We installed a small ballot box in a public hall lent by the municipality, where the employees could write small notes with the amount of share capital which each of them could invest. The collected sum was only €50,000. Thus, another €50,000 were needed.

One of the workers suggested that they go to the local community that was home both to the factory and to many of the workers themselves. So, in good grassroots fashion, they handed out information leaflets on the streets, collected money at the grocery store, knocked on people's door, and even stood with collection buckets on the highway near Ceralep. As one worker recalls:

> Those who gave us money were ordinary people, workers from other factories, passers-by, even a small child broke his piggy bank and gave us three euros. When I speak of it now, I still have gooseflesh. We collected between 5 and 50 euros per person. The supermarket across the road gave us 1,000 euros. They wanted Ceralep to remain alive, because there was a rumour that another supermarket would be built on our site. On top of that, they gave us food every day, so we could make lunch for all the workers in front of the factory gate for a few weeks. We also fed the guards who were keeping the gate. They discreetly allowed a handful of us to make shifts in the factory around the clock in order to maintain the machinery. Even the police were on our side. Once, the gendarmerie captain came and we shared sausages and coffee with him.

In fewer than ten days, 802 donors had together pledged a combined €50,000. Of course the story is much more complicated than what I am presenting. What I hope to convey to readers is that realizing both the spirit and the letter, so to speak—rules, contracts, agreements, orders—of the worker's cooperative is within their reach, too. The example of Ceralep shows the power of central cooperative tenets: community support, worker solidarity, horizontal decision-making, thorough transparency, shared income, in short, complete worker control.

I'd like briefly to mention two cooperatives that employ one of the most important anarchist strategies for creating expansive networks. This strategy is typically called "federation," the grouping together of allied, yet autonomous, organizations. The Desjardins Cooperative Group and the Mondragón Cooperative Group are two such examples. Comprised of over 81,000 workers, and with annual revenues in the tens of billions of dollars,[232] Mondragón, in Spain's Basque Autonomous Region, is a "horizontally integrated group of over 110 cooperative enterprises, involved in various industrial, service, financial, distribution, educational and research activities." As incredible as it may seem, Mondragón's numerous interconnected cooperatives operate wholly within the guidelines of the Statement on the Co-operative Identity of the International Co-operative Alliance:

> Cooperatives are based on the values of self-help, self-responsibility, democracy, equality, equity, and solidarity. In the tradition of their founders, cooperative members believe in the ethical values of honesty, openness, social responsibility and caring for others.[233]

In a statement that could have come from Peter Kroptokin, Javier Salaberria, the president of CICOPA, the world organization of

232 See "Mondragón Corporation Annual Report 2019," https://www.mondragon-corporation.com/2019urtekotxostena/?l=en. Accessed October 21, 2020.
233 International Co-operative Alliance. https://www.ica.coop/en/cooperatives/cooperative-identity. Accessed October 21, 2020.

industrial and service cooperatives, says, "Human beings are first of all cooperative beings. When they join together they become efficient." He also challenges the notion that Mondragón is an anomaly among cooperatives when he says, "I think that many aspects of the Mondragón culture can be transferred, and first of all its very strong practice of cooperation among cooperatives. It is possible to create many other Mondragóns, maybe smaller or even bigger."[234]

Desjardins, in Montreal, with annual revenues exceeding $188 billion, is another remarkable example of a large-scale, federated cooperative. Desjardins is a horizontally structured—that is, genuinely democratized and decentralized—banking cooperative comprised of 481 self-governing local cooperatives. In a recent analysis of the 500 largest financial institutions internationally, it is ranked in the top 50 of the most stable.[235] Given what we now know of the role that the finance sector's voracious greed played in the 2007 economic meltdown, it might surprise readers to learn this almost incredible fact: "Desjardins does not seek to maximize the return on investment to shareholders, but to ensure the financial service satisfaction of its 5.8 million owners–members, including 5.4 million individuals...and 400,000 enterprises."[236] Indeed, this cooperative approach insured that "Canada distinguish[ed] itself as being one of the most stable banking systems in the world."[237]

I will emphasize once again that none of the businesses highlighted here identifies as anarchist. Their values and approaches, however, are in close alignment with anarchism; and that is what matters. Let's review the values that drive these successful cooperatives: openness, honesty, and transparency; democracy, or one member, one vote; profit sharing; engaged social responsibility; equity and equality; horizontal, shared decision-making; in short, total ownership of one's labor.

To close this section, I would like to offer an account of my own

234 Bajo and Roelants, *Capital and the Debt Trap*, 211.

235 Bajo and Roelants, *Capital and the Debt Trap*, 152–153.

236 Bajo and Roelants, *Capital and the Debt Trap*, 152.

237 Bajo and Roelants, *Capital and the Debt Trap*, 174.

involvement in a worker cooperative, Incite Seminars, an educational cooperative in Philadelphia.[238] My aim, as throughout this manifesto, is to stimulate you to your own ideas about how you might form or refashion your project or business within an anarchist-inspired cooperative model.[239]

I started Incite Seminars in 2016. Since it is woven into the very fabric of the project, and informs the nature and direction of our programming, I should mention the direct impetus for its founding. That impetus was the rise of a destructive right-wing, overtly white supremacist, movement in America, coupled with a growing politics of regressive isolationist economic nationalism. Although the most recent manifestation of this tendency was the election of Donald Trump as president in 2016, it was clear that he was only the perverted figurehead of deeply rooted, long germinating American realities. The conditions of ignorance and hatred that enabled the Trump presidency will likely outlive his administration. You might be asking, well, why not get involved in politics? In classical anarchist fashion, I have always held the conviction that education *is* politics—it is decisive in forming the political subject in the world. Critically-oriented education, moreover, offers us a means to recognize, resist, and counter the forces of personal alienation and social division—forces such as hopelessness, bigotry, passivity, and self-delusion. For this reason, I conceived of Incite Seminars as a community of learners engaged in a vital *political* practice. Each seminar would be an experiential immersion in self-reflection, self-formation, and social critique. Through reading, thinking, and discussion, participants would come to realize unknown

---

238 See http://www.inciteseminars.com for more information.

239 Recall that such projects operate at the meso-level, where we, as individuals, form into the communities that make up the daily life of society. I imagine that meso structures relevant to my readers include the following: schools and colleges; workplaces, cafes, bookstores, offices; spaces of "spiritual" practice like meditation groups, yoga studios, churches and synagogues; places of healing, like doctor's offices, acupuncture clinics, message studios, chiropractor practices. Other examples might include, food co-ops, online learning networks, media and work collectives, day-care centers, neighborhood groups, rent and tenant associations, and so on. Can you think of others?

intellectual potentials, enhance interpersonal communication, and discover creative, effective ways of acting toward a genuinely just world.

Publicly, Incite Seminars does not loudly proclaim its anarchist orientation. This is for no other reason than projecting the fact that we want to maintain an open orientation to ideas. More importantly, as with the examples above, the essential matter is the values and strategies driving the cooperative. That being said, internally, the core team of workers who run the daily operations do tend toward an explicitly anarchist orientation. To require allegiance to anarchism, for either the worker-members or nonworker-members, however, would be wholly unnecessary; worse, it would be counterproductive.

So, what are those values? To name a few, we explicitly practice horizontal, shared decision-making. Although I founded Incite Seminars, I am not the "director." Such a model, typical, of course, for non-cooperative businesses, is "vertical," and entails the very hierarchies and inequalities that anarchism adamantly refuses to inscribe into its projects. This is not a mere stubborn ideological principle. We are an organization comprised of everyday workers, educators, scholars, writers, artists, musicians, poets, students, activists, of seekers and dreamers. Imagine the sheer wisdom, practical know-how, and wild creativity that would be dissipated within a vertical structure! Horizontality permits the free flow of input across the organization. This approach requires three additional values that I've mentioned: openness, honesty, and transparency. Again, it's not out of a desire to be virtuous that we hold these values. It's because they are necessary conditions for the circulation of intelligence and creativity. Why would any organization want to construct obstacles to its workers' imagination and desire? A special mention should be made of transparency. I have worked for one college, three universities, and one graduate institute in my life. Every one of them touted their "transparency." None of them was even remotely transparent. So, why did they bother to name it as a value? Just consider what it would mean to indicate, explicitly or by omission, that your organization is not transparent. "Opaque" and "blocked" are the antonyms that come to mind. And how apt they are! An organization that keeps hidden its *actual* processes for decision-making and all the rest is *necessarily* blocked—the creativity and intelligence of its workers cannot but be stifled and suffocated. At Incite Seminars, the core team is transparent to the point of sharing access to all of our accounts, including our website, social media, event management site, and credit union. Being transparent is an absolute condition, like being pregnant or being soaked. A half-measure transparency, furthermore, would require the presence of additional compromising values, such as authority, hierarchy, and inequality. Either these words mean what they say or nothing at all. One result of our transparency is that we review income at the beginning of each month and discuss how to distribute profits among workers. Honesty is essential here; otherwise resentments start building, and blockages occur. When these values are practiced, the result is genuine equity. Where there is equity, goodwill, enthusiasm, and satisfaction follow. Is this not a sensible model for building a business?

Compared to Natividad, Cerelap, Desjardins, and Mondragón, Incite Seminars is small. But we grow in membership and revenue every month. As an anarchist-oriented organization, it is essential to us that we *prefigure* the larger cooperative that we aspire to become. Recall that the strategy of prefiguration means that our approach and our goal must remain one and the same. To ensure that an organization is permeated by its values, those values must be lived, embodied, within every single act, every conversation, every decision, that the members engage. If, as a fresh, twenty-first century anarchist slogan has it, *a better world is possible,* it is because better people and better organizations are possible. I hope my readers have come some distance in agreeing that anarchism shows us a robust way.

Afterword

Anarchism: An Idea Whose Time Will Never Come?

When I opened the *New York Times* this morning, my eyes immediately fell on the headline: "With Billions at Stake, New York Sues Trump Over 'Anarchist' Label."[240] The administration is threatening to withhold $18 billion in federal funds because it deems New York City an "anarchist jurisdiction." It is a ludicrous claim, of course. The commerce capital of the world, the home to Wall Street, the place that, with $63 billion in yearly revenues, is more of a capitalist juggernaut than a human residence, an anarchist jurisdiction?[241] If only! Yet, what are we to make of the presence of a term that has barely been uttered in serious political or journalistic discourse in a century? A *New York Times* headline on September 30, 2020, reads "The Truth About Today's Anarchists," with the damning lede, "'Insurrectionary anarchists' have been protesting for racial justice all summer. Some Black leaders wish they would go home."[242] If those scare quotes are intended to soften the blow or, perhaps, complicate the accusation,

240 Farah Stockman, "With Billions at Stake, New York Sues Trump Over 'Anarchist' Label," *New York Times*, October 23, 2020.

241 A perusal of the "The City of New York Popular Annual Financial Report" for fiscal year 2019 certainly yields that impression. https://tinyurl.com/yx9cgjmq. Accessed October 23, 2020.

242 https://www.nytimes.com/2020/09/30/opinion/anarchists-protests-black-lives-matter.html

the World Socialist Web Site isn't having it. "*New York Times* echoes Trump's attacks on 'violent anarchists,'" the site proclaims, before echoing the perennial leftist perception of liberal-fascist collusion: "Stockman's [the author's] reactionary and false commentary has been warmly received by those on the far-right."[243] In a similar vein, scare quotes and all, the *Wall Street Journal* gives us, "'Anarchy' Is Not a New York City Crisis. It's a Lifestyle." The lede? "Critics who bemoan a 'decline' don't get it—this town happily embraces its chaos." A highlighted quote: "Anarchy is in the water here, like fluoride, and toilet alligators."[244] It is an extraordinarily puerile article. I felt embarrassed for the author, Jason Gay, as I read such ignorant, cliché-drenched, sarcasm-dripping lines as:

> My fellow anarchists of New York City:
>
> OK, it looks like the jig is up. The government is on to us. The White House recently labeled New York City an "anarchist jurisdiction," along with those felt-wearing, Teva-sniffers in Portland and Seattle.
>
> Come on! The first rule of New York City Anarchy Club is nobody talks about New York City Anarchy Club.
>
> Who squealed to the Feds?...
>
> This is a town that gave the world the chaotic greatness of the Ramones, Lou Reed, Public Enemy...This is town where jaywalking is a right, where a crosswalk is a mere suggestion, where real-estate agents show studio apartments with toilets in the kitchens, and, if you don't give a

---

243 Jacob Crosse, "*New York Times* echoes Trump's attacks on 'violent anarchists,'" World Socialist Web Site. https://www.wsws.org/en/articles/2020/10/03/stoc-o03.html. Accessed October 23, 2020.

244 Jason Gay, "'Anarchy' Is Not a New York City Crisis. It's a Lifestyle." https://www.wsj.com/articles/anarchy-is-not-a-new-york-city-crisis-its-a-lifestyle-11601645336. Accessed October, 23, 2020.

stranger a middle finger before 9 a.m., you're living completely wrong.

Is, in fact, anarchism an idea whose time will never come? As the scholarship shows, anarchism is a legitimate political philosophy, offering, as it does, a nuanced social analysis and critique coupled with a sophisticated social theory. As activists have proven, anarchism offers effective, pragmatic remedies to social ills. And as the builders of counter-institutions and cooperatives have shown us, anarchists are adept at creating viable alternatives to capitalism's unequal and unsustainable models. Indeed, all signs point to the fact that anarchism has the goods to be a force to be reckoned with in the world. So, why isn't it?

As the current resurgence of the term "anarchism" in mainstream discourse shows, no progress has been made since 1840 when Proudhon declared, "I am (in the full force of the term) an anarchist." Indeed, in its current usage, we have not progressed one inch from the 1500s when anarchism was defined as "unleful lyberty or lycence of the multytude," and it was universally declared that an anarchist is "one who upsets settled order."[245]

As I hope to have shown in this manifesto, these old definitions make a valid point. But it is not the valid point they think they are making. As an anarchist, I hold that my liberty is inviolable and non-negotiable. My liberty does not ensue from the "rights" granted me by the state. It is not a commodity that I can procure on the capitalist marketplace. It is not in need of government sanction or protection. Yes, it can, and constantly is, jeopardized, manipulated , and objectified by these human-created Golems. But it is unbound by and unbeholden to them. As anarchists, what is our basis for such an absolute claim? Do we ground our claim to inalienable liberty in "human nature"? Many early anarchists did so, but that move is neither common nor feasible today. Do we ground it some transcendent principle, like

245 See footnote 27.

Truth, Ultimate Reality, the Absolute, or God? Although we have had "spiritual" anarchists since the days of Tolstoy—people who weave Christianity, Buddhism, Paganism, Wicca, and other traditions into their anarchism—the prevailing motto seems to be "no gods, no masters." So, no; no transcendent grounding for our liberty. Rejecting the authority of the state, we obviously do not ground it in law, either. So, on what basis do anarchists declare that our liberty is inviolable? We ground it axiomatically. No discussion. No justification. Axiom: your liberty is inviolable.

> *axiom*, noun. From Latin *axioma*: that which is thought worthy, that which is assumed, a basis of demonstration, a principle.

Who among "the multytude" would not hold that an ungrounded, hence autonomous, notion of "liberty" is an eminently *worthy* notion? Stating this axiomatically does not, of course, make it so. We have, after all, renounced any natural, transcendent, legal, or other grounds for liberty. But in *assuming* it, in proceeding *as if*, we make it a principle on which we demonstrate new possibilities, new "planes of justification." We make it a principle on which to form *a life*, one that refuses, to the greatest extent possible, to fall into the preestablished ruts dictated by the powers and principalities of this world. Hence, the modifier "unleful" in the old yet disturbingly current definition. To be an anarchist is to grant *yourself* the license to create anew, to create otherwise, as you see fit. Doing so, you will quickly come to the perennial forked road of anarchism: individualism or socialism. Many anarchists have sought their liberty in isolation, removed as far as feasible from the tumult of the world. Others insist that we can run but not hide from one another, that the effects of the social whole—on our air and water, on geographical borders and divisions, on peace and war—are felt everywhere, and cannot but impact the individualist, even in the forests and the mountains. I personally have taken the collective, social, fork of the road. So, I believe that "liberty" is a social, rather than personal, attribute. That is, I cannot be free unless you are free.[246] Hence, the non-negotiable necessity to create actual material environments where anarchist values are lived and thereby proliferated throughout the world. Such individualist-socialist arguments aside, either way, doing so, granting yourself license, you will often appear to be operating "unlawfully" to some degree and to some extent. The laws of decorum, custom, and received "wisdom" are as binding as those of the courts. You will find yourself in a strange, uncomfortable position, outside the status quo, outside, that is, of the existing state of affairs. When you do, take comfort in the fact that those who, dreaming of a better world, fought for such quixotic absurdities as the end of slavery, the eight-hour workday, the abolishment of child labor, a cure for tuberculosis, mandatory recycling, a black U.S. president, women's suffrage, or, indeed, the end to the divine right of kings, and countless other once unassailable realities—stand in solidarity with you.

When we meditate on the state of world, when we simply acknowledge its interminable injustice, cruelty, desecration, division, and violence, how can we, each one of us, not aspire to become "one who upsets settled order"? Anarchism is the most adaptive, humane, intelligent, singly inclusive proposal that we, as social animals, have ever envisioned.

---

246 I believe that humans cannot be free unless animals are free as well. In fact, I subscribe to the concept of "total liberation." As Steven Best says in *The Politics of Total Liberation: Revolution for the 21st Century*, "We must reject partial struggles for a broader, deeper, more complex, and more inclusive concept [of solidarity and liberation] and politics...We need to build a revolutionary movement strong enough to vanquish capitalist hegemony and to remake society without [the] crushing loadstones of anthropocentrism, speciesism, patriarchy, racism, classism, statism, heterosexism, ableism, and every other pernicious form of hierarchal domination." Google Books, no page numbers. https://tinyurl.com/y55cv6pk. Accessed October 23, 2020.

About the Author

Glenn Wallis holds a Ph.D. in Buddhist Studies from Harvard University's Department of Sanskrit and Indian Studies. Prior to that, he studied at the renowned Institute for Indology and Buddhist Studies at the University of Göttingen, Germany. Wallis has published widely on various aspects of Buddhism. His books are *A Critique of Western Buddhism: Ruins of the Buddhist Real; Cruel Theory|Sublime Practice: Toward a Revaluation of Buddhism* (with contributions from Tom Pepper and Matthias Steingass); *Buddhavacana: A Pali Reader; Basic Teachings of the Buddha; The Dhammapada: Verses on the Way;* and *Mediating the Power of Buddhas: Ritual in the Mañjuśrīmūlakalpa.* His most recent book, *How to Fix Education: A Handbook for Direct Action,* was published by Warbler Press.

Wallis taught in the religion departments of Brown University, Bowdoin College, and the University of Georgia. In 2006, he gave up tenure to initiate an innovative meditation program at the newly formed Won Institute of Graduate Studies, near Philadelphia. The program trained professionals (teachers, psychologists, nurses, social workers, etc.) to incorporate meditation programs into their work. It emphasized the interconnected necessity for individual and collective solutions to social ills.

In 2011, Wallis founded the groundbreaking blog Speculative Non-Buddhism (www.speculativenonbuddhism.com), which one critic considers "the most strikingly original, penetrating, and provocative writing about Buddhism on the web." To date, the blog has published over 120 long-form critical essays. Its notorious comment section houses over 7,000 comments. With views approaching one million, this influential blog has been written about in several scholarly books and articles, and on numerous online sites.

Currently, Wallis co-directs Incite Seminars (www.inciteseminars.com), the counterinstituional educational cooperative he founded in Philadelphia in 2016. As its tagline, "rigorous & rebellious learning," indicates, Incite Seminars offers spirited public courses on topics relevant to its aim of upsetting the status quo toward a better world for all sentient beings.

Acknowledgements

This book owes its existence to Mary Bahr of Warbler Press. A year before an American president reinfected our collective consciousness with fear of "radical left-wing anarchists," Mary had the prescience to realize the timeliness of the topic. She has nurtured this work with a quality of care and intelligence that would hearten any writer. Like Mary, Warbler Press itself radiates the egalitarian creative spirit of anarchism. Thank you!

I also want to acknowledge the Anarchist Reading Circle at Incite Seminars. I was able to put many of the ideas in this text before the kinds of compassionate, intelligent, and comradely people one encounters in anarchist communities.

This is also to acknowledge the fact that no work—no book, no piece of art, no organization or institution—is the accomplishment of a single individual. Multitudes have come before me. May this book be a vessel for their passionate struggle for a just world.

I am only able to do this work because of the support of Friederike Baer, my wife and life companion. She provides the emotional and material ground on which I conduct my intellectual explorations. Best of all, she accompanies me on the way, pointing out surprising vistas and untrodden pathways.

www.ingramcontent.com/pod-product-compliance
Lightning Source LLC
Chambersburg PA
CBHW022337280326
41934CB00006B/666